Florida

IN THE

Great Depression

DESPERATION AND DEFIANCE

Nick Wynne & Joseph Knetsch

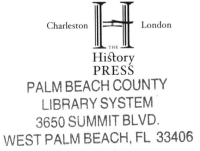

Charleston — London

THE
History
PRESS

Published by The History Press
Charleston, SC 29403
www.historypress.net

First published 2012

Manufactured in the United States

ISBN 978.1.60949.806.1

Library of Congress CIP data applied for.

For Debra Chapin Wynne and Linda Knetsch.

With a special dedication to the late Sybil Bray, Sarah Nell Gran, Celeste Kavanaugh and Warren Weekes—all gone but never forgotten.

CONTENTS

INTRODUCTION

For six to seven years after the end of World War I, Florida was the envy of every state in the Union. Millions of dollars flowed into the state's economy as dreamer after dreamer tried to outdo each other in building new towns and communities. Some of these men were true visionaries, motivated by their desires to do something worthwhile and to leave lasting memorials to their aspirations and to themselves. Others, however, were "fast buck artists," motivated solely by a desire to make money at the expense of trusting souls. Together, scammers and dreamers combined to make real estate in the Sunshine State the hottest commodity in the world.

When the end of the boom came in 1926–27, Florida was hard hit, perhaps more so than other states, simply because so many individuals had abandoned their home states—with the built-in security systems of family and friends—to come south and seek their fortunes. Miami, which had been the Mecca for speculators, celebrities and con men, was particularly hard hit. As historian Arva Moore Parks McCabe has written, "Miami was the first in [the Depression], but also the first out." Watching events unfold in Miami, Tampa and Jacksonville during the 1930s provides a window on how urban Floridians survived. Although Florida had become a largely urban state by 1930, there were still significant numbers of residents in rural areas, and the experiences of these Floridians were radically different than those of their city-dwelling cousins.

With the unfolding of Franklin Delano Roosevelt's New Deal programs, rural and urban areas of the Sunshine State underwent additional changes.

INTRODUCTION

By 1935, Florida had received money through myriad "alphabet agencies," all with different approaches to solving the problem of unemployment but infusing millions of federal dollars into the state's economy. Trying to make sense of these agencies is guaranteed to give the average person a horrendous headache, since many of them changed focus and names during the 1930s. We have tried to simplify our discussions of these agencies, retaining some original names and separating some smaller agencies from their larger parent organizations.

Among the most important aspects of the Great Depression in Florida are the ways it impacted traditional labor patterns, race relations and expectations. As one elderly Floridian recently remarked in a conversation with the authors, "We changed because we had to, but we managed to survive, and that's what is important!"

The Depression ended in 1942, not so much because of the variety of "make-work" programs as the demands for fighting a world war on several fronts. For many Floridians, the trauma of the Great Depression was replaced by the larger trauma of seeing an entire generation go to war, just twenty or so years after the end of World War I.

Florida historians seldom work alone, and much of the material in this book rightly belongs to Arva Moore Parks McCabe, Sandra Thurlow, Patsy West, Toni Collins, Tom Knowles, Jody Miller, Dr. Linda Pulliam, Laura Baas, Miriam Spaulding, Dr. Brian Rucker, Bill Howell, Deborah Mekeel, Claude Kenneson, Pam Gibson, Jim Schnur, John and Eleanor Thrasher, Alyce Tincher and Linden Lindsey. Ben Dibiase of the Florida Historical Society Library in Cocoa was also helpful. Thank you all.

Chapter 1

A PERFECT PARADISE:
1920–1926

*The greatest of all Florida's resources is the fertility of its agricultural lands.
Every intelligent investor in Florida property realizes that the value of his
investment is in a large measure based upon the development of the State's
agricultural resources.*
—*Frank Parker Stockbridge and John Holliday Perry,*
Florida in the Making *(1926)*

Recently, Florida historian Gary R. Mormino published a social history of Florida with the title *Land of Sunshine, State of Dreams*—an apt description of the Sunshine State in the post–World War II era. Mormino was not the first to take note of the perpetual state of dreams that seems to dominate any discussion about Florida, although his descriptions are more balanced than most. In 1926, at the height of the Florida land boom, Frank Parker Stockbridge and John Holliday Perry published a lengthy book called *Florida in the Making*, which gave a rosy, Chamber of Commerce picture of the Sunshine State and its potential for future growth. Of the state's thirty-five million acres, fewer than two million were under cultivation by some fifty thousand farmers, who produced crops (peanuts, tobacco, velvet beans and corn) valued at more than $80 million in the open market. In addition, Florida farmers possessed beef cattle valued at $25 million, horses and mules worth $14 million, hogs valued at $6 million and additional mixed livestock worth $4.5 million. Florida farmlands were valued at an average of $109.76 per acre, which greatly exceeded the value of comparable lands

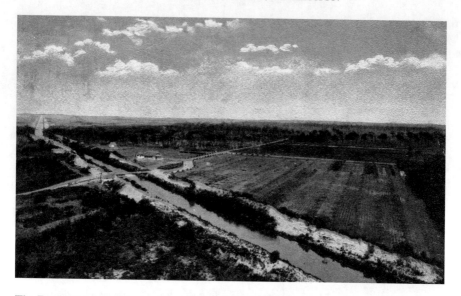

The Everglades, long home to the mysterious Seminole Indians, was opened to muck farming in the 1920s and 1930s and was seen as the salvation of Florida farming. *Courtesy of the Wynne Collection.*

in other states. For example, the value of farmland in the "breadbasket" midwestern states was significantly lower, as in Iowa ($12.22 per acre), Ohio ($13.36 per acre) and Illinois ($12.48 per acre). Florida farmers were so successful that the failure rate, or percentage of bankruptcies, was "13.4 percent below the average in the United States." There appeared to be no limits to agricultural prosperity in the state, and the men ballyhooed the fact that twenty million acres of fertile, virgin soil remained on the Florida peninsula just waiting for farmers bold enough to take advantage of the opportunity to purchase and plant.

Farmers were not the only individuals who were prospering in the Sunshine State. According to Stockbridge and Perry, an additional eleven million acres were covered with pine timber, available for harvesting as lumber or for cultivation for naval stores. Each year, more than $30 million of lumber was sold. In 1926, the overheated building boom of residential housing throughout the state held nothing but the promise of higher and higher sales. Although yellow pine was the principal source of lumber in Florida, cypress, oak, red gum and black gum trees were also harvested in great numbers.

Turpentine production, commonly referred to as the naval stores industry, was centered in northern Florida, and the number of trees

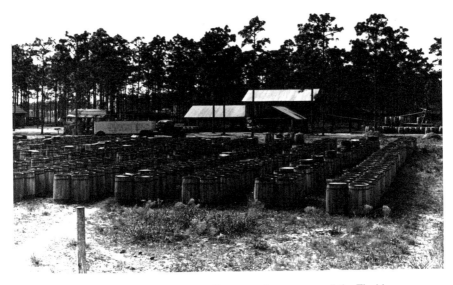

Logging and naval stores were major contributors to the economy of the Florida Panhandle, but when available forests ran out and the demand for turpentine collapsed, these industries suffered greatly. *Courtesy of the Library of Congress.*

bearing "cat faces" (where the bark had been removed to make the sap flow) was in the millions. The annual output was valued at $20 million. Pine trees, whether tapped for resin or cut for lumber, were listed as Florida's greatest natural resource, but even Stockbridge and Perry added a cautionary note: "How long it will be before the pine forests are denuded no one can estimate. It is hardly likely that any comprehensive plan of reforestation will be generally adopted."

Citrus growing received its plaudits as well. The Sunshine State could count almost ten million orange and grapefruit trees in 1926. That number encompassed just the fruit-bearing trees that were commercially viable and did not take into account an additional thirty million trees that comprised nursery stock and untended groves. In 1925, the Florida commissioner of markets reported that Florida citrus had produced an aggregate of $51,469,280 in gross revenue on sales of 19,171,440 boxes of fruit. Even with these positive figures, the Sunshine State still ranked second behind California, where effective advertising, lower shipping costs and cooperative selling offset the better taste of Florida citrus. The authors of *Florida in the Making* predicted that California's advantages were temporary and would quickly be overcome by applying the same techniques to Florida citrus crops.

Agriculture was not the only aspect of the Florida economy that was on the upswing. Gross annual income for beef cattle alone rose from

$2,383,000 in 1925 to $3,221,000 in 1926, and projections for 1927 were that the industry would increase its annual income by several millions of dollars. Hog producers, fishermen and dairy farmers enjoyed similar leaps in prosperity, and their expectations for rising income were equally high. So too were the owners of phosphate mines and other extractive industries in the Sunshine State.

The problem with the statistics ballyhooing the success of agriculture, the forest products industries and livestock production was that these figures represented the successes of large corporate farms and livestock operations. By the mid-1920s, the face of rural Florida was beginning to change; small, family-owned farms of two or three hundred acres were failing, and specialized corporations began to acquire large tracts of land. These large farms depended on an abundance of cheap labor, most of which was provided by the former owners, who became tenant farmers, or by the large and property-less African American population, which

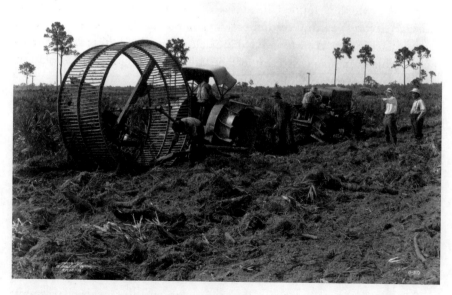

Massive machines were used to clear brush and trees from the Everglades muck lands. Where only scrub brush and trees once dominated the landscape, miles of neat rows of beans and other vegetables soon were under cultivation. *Courtesy of the Burgert Brothers Collection, Tampa Public Library.*

worked as wage labor or sharecroppers. Slowly, the best farmlands were consolidated into large corporate operations, leaving small, independent farmers to try to make a living on marginal lands, paying top dollar for seed and supplies while the larger operations enjoyed the benefits of buying and selling in bulk.

It was speculation in raw land, however, that received the most publicity and seemed to be an unlimited source of money to expand the state's economy. The list of wealthy investors in Florida land was a who's who of the rich and powerful. Financial luminaries Barron C. Collier, John D. Rockefeller, Henry Ford and Harvey Firestone headed a long list of investors who commissioned the purchases of millions of acres of raw land. Purchasing undeveloped land in the Sunshine State was "a game for capitalists, and a list of capitalists who have invested and are still investing in Florida land would be almost a transcript of the 'Directory of Directors,'" wrote Stockbridge and Perry. Kahn, Vanderbilt, Dahlberg, Heckscher, Ruppert, Babson, Du Pont, Conners and Ringling were just some of the names—less known today but familiar to the public in the 1920s—that showed up on deed transfers. Although the actual sum of money paid for raw land was impossible to know exactly, knowledgeable authorities estimated the total spent in 1925 at more than $450 million. None of the other purchases of land exceeded that of Collier—his 1,050,000 acres became the basis for two new counties in the Sunshine State. These investors were, according to Stockbridge and Perry, "men of wealth who are still betting that the Florida 'boom' is not only not over, but that it is just beginning."

Not all investments were in raw land. In many places in the state, men with visions of newly created towns and subdivisions hurriedly amassed large parcels and sent in the bulldozers to clear brush and build roads. George E. Merrick (Coral Gables), Addison Mizner (Boca Raton), Carl Fisher (Miami Beach), Glenn Hammond Curtiss (Hialeah) and D.P. Davis (Davis Islands) were the stars of this movement to create towns out of whole cloth, but they were merely the leading lights of several hundred developers. Joseph W. Young Jr. was one of the lesser-known visionaries, but his Hollywood-by-the-Sea attracted a wealthy clientele who shared his dream of a Florida center for moviemaking, while merchandiser J.C. Penney created Penney Farms in 1926 as a community for retired Christian ministers and lay workers. Still other developments were designed to provide havens for aficionados of golf, and still others, such as Howey-in-the-Hills and Temple Terrace, became Meccas for gentleman citrus farmers. Like the "men of wealth," although with less money, these entrepreneurs were betting that the boom was not over but just beginning.

So much money was being poured into the Sunshine State that it attracted, like bees to the honey pot, those individuals who wanted to be seen as part of the nonstop action of the frenzied lifestyles of the rich, near rich and wannabe rich. Movie stars, professional and top amateur athletes, major crime figures, petty criminals, preachers, teachers and titled Europeans followed the railroads south to Florida, some in private rail cars filled with servants and all the trappings of money, while others hitched illegal rides on passing freights carrying only what they could carry on their backs. Still others came in their yachts or motorcars, navigating the 2,200 miles of paved roads of which Florida officials were so proud. They came in droves, rapidly pushing the population of the state above the one million mark for the first time, all seeking their share of the paradise that developers and state agencies promised was available for the taking.

Newly elected Governor John W. Martin embraced the "no inheritance tax and no income tax" amendment to the state constitution, which was advocated by Governor Cary A. Hardee, passed by the legislature and ratified in the general election of 1924. It was, Martin argued, a necessary tool to attract more new developers and more and richer citizens to the state. The Florida State Chamber of Commerce even published a leaflet outlining the legal steps necessary to become a permanent Florida resident in order to take advantage of the state's tax haven status. Prohibiting inheritance and income taxes was just the first step in reshaping the Sunshine State pro-investment image. In 1925, the legislature revamped the laws governing incorporation to allow the quick and effortless creation of new companies. It also passed new laws to regulate real estate brokers and citrus sales and established the speed limit in the Sunshine State at forty-five miles per hour, while prohibiting municipalities from setting any limit below twenty-five miles an hour. This was the highest legal speed limit in the United States. One wag remarked that Floridians wanted nothing to "slow down the danged fools bringing money into the state."

Making money was the bottom line for newcomers and old-line residents. Across the state, banks sprouted like weeds in the field. Poorly regulated, undercapitalized and often regarded as the personal piggy banks for the incorporators, the Sunshine State could count 54 national banks and 162 state banks in 1925. Miami alone boasted 1 national bank and 14 state banks. Bank deposits in Florida totaled $199,589,122 in 1920, and by mid-1925 deposits had reached the staggering sum of $575,758,195. This tripling of

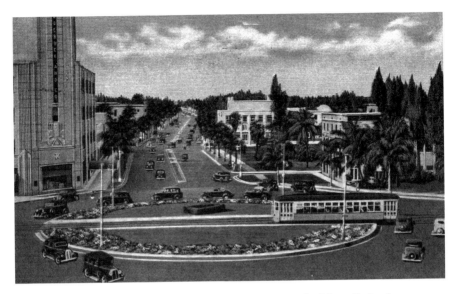

Miami was the epicenter of the 1920s land boom. It became the Mecca for land speculators, dreamers and celebrities of the boom era. When the boom collapsed, Miami's economy was particularly hard hit. *Courtesy of Arva Parks McCabe.*

deposits represented "nearly $450 for every man, woman and child, Indians and Negroes included, enumerated in the State census of 1925." Stockbridge and Perry were quick to remind their readers that "like everything else in Florida, it is outside of all human experience, almost unbelievable, because so utterly unfamiliar that those who have not seen Florida with their own eyes have no standard whereby to measure it."

In every aspect of human endeavor, the Sunshine State could boast institutions on par with those of any nation in the world. The system of higher education—crowned by the all-male State University at Gainesville and the all-female Florida State College for Women in Tallahassee—was improved by the expansion of Rollins College in Winter Park and Stetson College in DeLand. In 1922, Southern College, a coeducational college supported by the Southern Methodist Conference, relocated from Clearwater to Lakeland, its present home. Palmer College, a Presbyterian college, thrived in DeFuniak Springs in the Panhandle. In 1925, George Merrick announced the establishment of the University of Miami as part of his Coral Gables development.

In 1925, Florida could boast of 32 daily newspapers, with some cities having several, and 126 weekly or monthly newspapers. The *Miami Daily News*, owned by James A. Cox, claimed a world record when it published a single edition in 1925 that contained 504 pages, mostly advertising for housing developments and land sales. Its competitor, the *Miami Herald*, owned by Frank B. Shutts, claimed its own record in 1925, when it published more lines of advertising than any other newspaper in the world. Journalistic success became a function of advertising dollars, not news reporting.

As the influx of new residents grew, cities and towns developed amenities that marked them as sites for cultural development. Movie theaters, many of which were among the first to be air conditioned in the United States, became a staple in virtually all towns, while small orchestras and acting troupes added the leavening that made the cultural life in the Sunshine State equal to that in any other state. The Chautauqua movement enjoyed a modest revival in Florida, and some adherents made annual pilgrimages to DeFuniak Springs, Cocoa and numerous other small towns. As quickly as they were created, the new towns and developments in the Sunshine State took on a veneer of civilization.

Truly, Florida at the beginning of 1926 was publicly portrayed as being as close to paradise as mortals could make it. In the last chapter of *Florida in the Making*, the authors begin with this statement: "The question which skeptics are asking everywhere is 'When will the Florida boom collapse?'" Although Stockbridge and Perry pooh-poohed the idea that the boom would ever end, it was a question that deserved serious consideration without the overarching umbrella of their hubris.

Chapter 2

HARBINGERS OF
HARD TIMES

I deposit[ed] *some money in the Ocala Metropolitan Saving Bank private for safe keeping, in a private Box, and I and then also my child had some money in that Bank on checking account and the bank is closed and they will not pay me any of the money*[.] *They say I cant get it.*
—*Julia B. Timmons to Governor Doyle E. Carlton, November 12, 1929.*
Quoted in Elna C. Green's Looking for the New Deal: Florida Women's Letters during the Great Depression

Although private investors, state officials and pro-business organizations dedicated an enormous amount of time and energy to touting Florida's land boom and future economic potential, the reality was that even as statistics reflected massive monetary growth, the foundations of the state's economy were beginning to collapse. Florida's growth was akin to the gigantic oak trees that flourished in the Sunshine State, where outward appearances were not reliable indicators of weak root systems nor was sheer size evidence of healthy growth. As Florida natives could attest, such trees often collapsed under their own weight or fell to the winds of tropical storms or hurricanes. Such was the state's economy—healthy by every known indicator but ready to collapse for the slightest of reasons. As early as August 1925, when the Florida East Coast (FEC) Railroad announced an embargo on shipments of building materials and other nonperishable goods, the boom was over, although few people recognized the fact. The failure of developers to build adequate warehouse facilities and to offload cargoes, tying up the FEC rolling

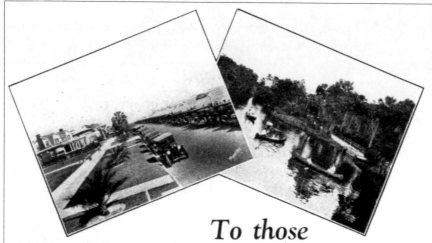
Despite the problems of overcrowding and the difficulties in procuring building materials
and food, land promoters continued to tout the money to be made in purchasing Florida
lands. *Courtesy of the Burgert Brothers Collection, Tampa Public Library.*

stock, meant that the railroad faced a shortage of cars and a dramatic loss of income. The failure to develop adequate port facilities meant that ships carrying materials waited outside Florida ports for weeks at a time, waiting for an opportunity to offload. Outside the port of Miami in December 1925, some thirty-one ships lay at anchor waiting. To make matters worse, the ship *Prinz Valdemar*, which was being renovated as a floating casino, sank and blocked the channel that led to the docks. It took engineers more than two months to dig another channel around the sunken ship. In the meantime, housing construction ground to a halt because of the lack of materials. The few materials available brought substantially higher prices than they had just a few months earlier. The collapse had started.

Although the FEC enforced its embargo on nonperishable cargoes, it did nothing to halt the flow of people to the Sunshine State. Finding housing and foodstuffs for the constantly growing population placed inordinate demands on the transportation systems of Florida. Despite the difficulties brought about by the rail embargo, nothing slowed the inexorable movement of people to the state.

Land sales began a precipitous decline by early 1926. The actual figures for the decline are hard to come by, but a reliable estimate can be obtained from bank records. In December 1925, state and national banks reported resources of $943 million, but by mid-1926, deposits fell by more than $300 million. More than 40 banks, including 1 national bank, closed their doors as they sought to deal with the financial crisis. Although about half of these banks reorganized and reopened, the failures created a growing distrust of banks in Florida. Historian Charlton Tebeau noted that these failures did not bring an immediate halt to the banking business and cited the fact that "enough new banks opened in the state to make a net gain in the number that year of four national and ten state banks." Bank regulators, drinking the same Kool-Aid as other state officials, made notes on banking irregularities but failed to recommend closure or other drastic measures to strengthen failing banks. Some used their influence as regulators to secure positions in the very same banks they were supposed to police. The rot had set in, and soon this lack of forceful supervision would bring about a general collapse of banking in the Sunshine State. Between 1925 and 1934, 45 national banks and 171 state banks with combined assets of $131 million on their books failed.

Cities, counties and special tax districts were also in financial trouble. In order to pay for improvements such as roads, sewers, water systems and electrical grids, these political entities issued more than $600 million in bonds. In 1926, the first bond default occurred, followed quickly in 1927, 1928 and 1929 by numerous other defaults. As the boom in land sales and home construction ended, collection of outstanding property taxes (which were the basis for bond repayment) came to a standstill. Half-finished subdivisions and partially completed houses lay abandoned in the hot Florida sun as owners found it impossible to meet their mortgages and tax obligations. Schoolteachers and other public employees were forced to accept scrip in lieu of cash for their services, and so too were thousands of employees in private businesses. Those individuals who had cash reserves held on to what they had, which contributed to a further constriction of the economy. Fewer unnecessary purchases were made, and average citizens came to learn firsthand what words like "foreclosure" and "repossession" meant. By the onset of the Great Depression in 1929, Floridians had long been accustomed to trying to survive in a decaying economy.

The state government, which had expanded its annual budget for road construction and schools during the boom, now faced a critical situation of not being able to meet its obligations on time. Declining revenues made it necessary to curtail capital expenditures by mid-1926 until additional monies could be found from new tax sources. Given the increasing number of automobiles in the state, increased taxes on gasoline was a favorite device for raising funds. The legislature, charged with funding the state's budget, considered a multitude of other taxing methods over the next few years, including legalizing pari-mutuel betting and taxing the process. Successive legislative sessions considered this taxing proposal, and after much political jockeying, it became law on June 3, 1931, over the veto of Governor Doyle E. Carlton, who had followed John W. Martin in the governor's chair in 1929.

John Wellborn Martin, who was elected governor in 1925 just as the boom was ending, nevertheless worked hard to keep it going. Utilizing the various state agencies, he sponsored a deluge of propaganda pamphlets that touted the continuing prosperity of the Sunshine State. In October 1925, Martin attended a conference in New York City where he assured skeptics that investors "will do better in Florida than elsewhere because the State offers them easily four times the opportunity to which they are accustomed." Although he sought to convince others of the stability of the boom, Martin had the misfortune to preside over the state when the crazy patchwork of speculative investments came crashing down.

The banking crisis of 1925 was merely the first symptom of the financial disaster that awaited the Sunshine State. By February 1926, the

Harbingers of Hard Times

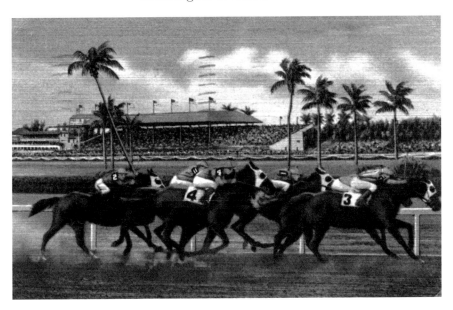

Horse racing, a favorite sport for Florida newcomers, provided the government of the Sunshine State with millions of dollars when pari-mutuel betting was approved in 1931. *Courtesy of the Wynne Collection.*

dollar value of outstanding obligations on land and subdivisions exceeded the total amount of money in circulation in the state. Large investors and individual homeowners found it increasingly difficult to meet their obligations to lending institutions, while nervous depositors sought to preserve their monies by withdrawing them from the banks. With each new rumor of a bank in difficulty, confidence in the banking system fell to new lows. The economic miracle of the Sunshine State was based on a rickety, shifting foundation.

It is difficult to determine whether or not the Florida boom could have survived the upheavals in the state's banking system. It never really got the chance. On September 17 and 18, 1926, an unnamed category four hurricane slammed into the southern end of the peninsula, killing 392 persons, injuring some 6,000 more and leaving a path of destruction across the state. The damage from the storm was immense; only a few buildings in Miami and Miami Beach were left intact, and the destruction continued as the storm moved westward into the Gulf of Mexico. After crossing the Gulf, the hurricane made landfall again in the Panhandle before moving on to Mobile, Alabama. The toll for the storm was estimated at $100 million, which, adjusted for today's dollars, would amount to $1.31 billion.

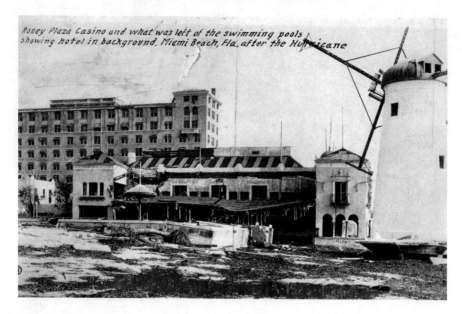

Miami and Miami Beach experienced severe damage from the hurricane of September 17, 1926, but few boosters of the growing city saw the hurricane as a harbinger of the end of the building boom. *Courtesy of the Wynne Collection.*

Although Governor Martin and other state and county officials were reluctant to discuss the economic impact of the hurricane, the public at large was left with the impression that Florida was a hurricane magnet, attracting destructive storms on a regular basis. Some officials, such as the mayor of Miami and Tampa civic leader Peter O. Knight, downplayed the storm's impact and refused assistance from outside the state. For these men, any negative publicity was to be quickly squashed so that the state's tourism industry and land boom could continue unhampered. Denial would prove fruitless, however, and both tourism and development slowed precipitously. As Charlton Tebeau wrote in his *A History of Florida*, "The 1926 blow did not kill the boom, but it certainly buried it in devastating fashion."

Some developers, like Miami Beach developer Carl Fisher, struggled on, but for others like George Edgar Merrick, the force behind Coral Gables, the storm was simply too much to overcome. Merrick, whose development was funded by loans from insurance companies, found that his funding sources were hard pressed to pay the myriad damage claims generated by the hurricane, and he was forced to abandon his Coral Gables project. Within a year, Merrick was reduced to operating a small fishing camp in the Florida Keys. Even independently wealthy Carl Fisher, who had also expended large

Harbingers of Hard Times

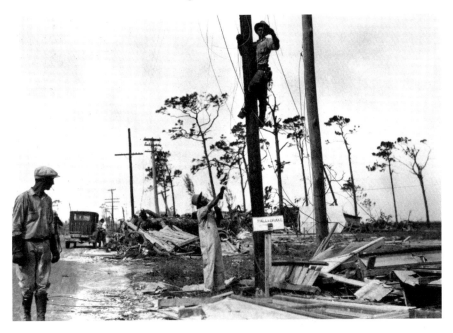

Linemen work to restore electricity to south Florida homes in the wake of the September 1926 hurricane, which caused some $100 million (in 1926 dollars) in damage. *Courtesy of the Wynne Collection.*

sums on developing a Long Island equivalent of Miami Beach, could sustain his operations for only a short time before he too simply ran out of money. David Paul "Doc" Davis, another of the major developers, had invested the millions he made from his Davis Islands project in Tampa in a new development in St. Augustine and managed to hang on for a while. On October 12, 1926, just a year later, he disappeared while on an ocean voyage to Europe aboard the liner *Majestic*. Some people speculated that Davis engineered his disappearance to collect on a $300,000 insurance policy, while others argued that his death was the result of drunken horseplay. Still others have advanced the idea of a suicide caused by despondency over the collapse of the boom. Whatever the cause, Davis was gone.

The financial disasters faced by large-scale developers were the best known collapses of the boom, but the failures of men like Davis, Merrick and Fisher were played out hundreds of times in other locations in the Sunshine State but on lesser scales. In posh Vero Beach, Anne Keen noted in a 1987 interview, "[The] Depression hit hard. Mother and Dad had friends in the real estate business who lost everything and had to move away. Everything [was] on paper. [We] hit bottom here." In neighboring Brevard County, attorney Gus Edwards,

23

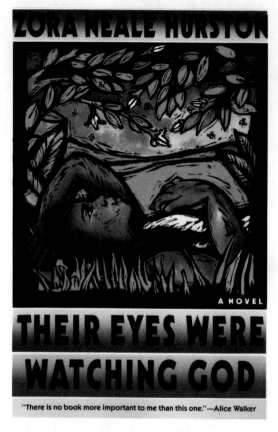

"There is no book more important to me than this one."—Alice Walker

Zora Neale Hurston's *Their Eyes Were Watching God*, published in 1937, was a graphic account of the 1928 hurricane and its impact on the thousands of migrant workers in the bean fields of south Florida. *Courtesy of the Wynne Collection.*

who had purchased large parcels of land on the barrier island east of Cocoa and who wanted to create a new Palm Beach or Miami Beach, found it difficult to sell any building lots—he would have to wait until the space race of the 1960s to make any profit at all. In nearby Rockledge, the modest boom enjoyed by architect Richard Rummell and builder C. Sweet Smith slowed and eventually dried up. Throughout the Sunshine State, small subdivisions baked in the Florida sun, unfinished and unoccupied.

It was difficult for the state's political and business leaders to grasp the fact that the boom was over, and they continued to promote continued investments in land and development. On September 16, 1928, the undeniable end to the boom came when the Sunshine State was lashed by another major hurricane, more devastating than that of 1926. When it finally exited the state, several thousand people were dead and estimates of the casualties ranged from 1,770 by the Red Cross to more than 2,000 by the Department of Commerce. More recent studies place the toll at more than 10,000, although exact figures are not available. Many bodies were washed into the swamps, fields and forests only to be found later, unaccounted for and uncounted. Although many of the dead were Bahamian immigrants or poor migrant workers who worked the cane fields or truck farms, the death toll—real or estimated—cast a pall on Florida's reputation as the American paradise.

Harbingers of Hard Times

Natural disaster followed natural disaster. On December 30, 1928, a severe freeze hit the Sunshine State, and thousands of acres of beans almost ready to be picked were destroyed. Three months later, infestations of the Mediterranean fruit fly were found in all the major citrus-producing groves in the state. Some twenty thousand unemployed men were hired to destroy infected trees. Commercial citrus production fell dramatically, falling from twenty-eight million boxes shipped in 1928–1929 to a low of eighteen million boxes shipped in 1930. In a 1969 interview, Pernell Kennedy of Indian River County recalled, "Well, citrus was prominent [in the county], of course, nothing like it is today, but it was prominent. Everyone was having a tough time then. I mean, it was hard to get anything for your citrus." Employees of the State Department of Agriculture estimated that the citrus industry would take ten years to fully recover.

Elsewhere in the Sunshine State, cattlemen were faced with a double plague—Texas ticks and a new disease, the screwworm. Beef prices fell, and Florida cattle were quarantined from the major market in Cuba. In north and central Florida, tobacco and cotton farmers faced threats from insects such as cutworms and boll weevils.

Perhaps, mused one Floridian, all of the disasters visited on the state were payments for all the bragging and ballyhooing that had dominated the boom years. Perhaps.

Chapter 3

POLITICS, POLITICS AND MORE POLITICS

I have but followed our President's wise example which in his own words was substituting food for words, work for idleness, hope for despair.
—David Sholtz, governor of Florida

The politics of the 1920s in Florida were beset with cronyism, corruption and nepotism. Banker-governor Cary Hardee set a number of his associates up in governmental positions at relatively high wages and often ran the state's business from his home offices in Live Oak, where he remained president of the local bank. Lawyer John Martin did not question the unparalleled growth of the state in population, wealth and growth during the boom times. Apparently stuck in the furor of the frenzied land boom, he saw little reason to look beyond the bank statements and multiplying subdivisions that signaled the transition of Florida from a rural, agricultural society into a new urbanized state, complete with the common problems of urbanization: transportation problems, infrastructure construction and housing—especially among minorities. Although the 1926 hurricane should have been ample warning that things were about to change, Martin and those around him ignored the signs and blithely moved ahead. Even when the next storm shook the Everglades in 1928, the governor appeared complacent and did not swing into action until after the federal government, the Florida National Guard and many local governments had already done so. As noted by Eliot Kleinberg in his book *Black Cloud: The Great Florida Hurricane of 1928*, when the governor was notified about the early reports of devastation, he simply informed the head of the Florida National Guard that he would think about sending the Guard, but he did not think the damage would be severe. Like the coverup regarding the outbreak of smallpox in 1926, anything that would damage the spirit of investment and growth was to be dampened, smothered or obliterated. Gaudiness, greed and growth were the bywords of the mid-1920s, and Martin, Ernest Amos and others were not going to be the cause of any downswing in the activity.

Hurricanes, smallpox, the lack of a transportation infrastructure and a poorly run banking establishment doomed the boom. Even by the time Martin took office, signs of the impending slowdown were on the horizon. The state had passed constitutional limitations on inheritance taxes, banned income taxes and basically ran its very limited government on the proverbial shoestring. Licensing fees, low property taxes and a gas tax similar to that put forth in New York by Governor Franklin D. Roosevelt were the major source of tax revenue to run the government. The legislature only met every other year, and the governor and cabinet ran the government during the interim. Bluntly stated, the government of Florida was too small, outdated and completely unable to handle anything of substance. When the nationwide depression began, the weak government of the state was in no shape to handle such a downturn.

The state had already entered a strong downturn in 1925–26 when the hurricane put an exclamation point on the state of affairs. Because so many of the railroads in the state were single-track and the road system was still under construction (with the aid of leftover World War I surplus machines), the transportation of housing materials and other needed supplies was lacking when needed most. Subdivisions took much of the usable lands near the growing urban centers, making the more marginal lands farther out from the cities and towns the focus of new farms, many of which were unsuitable for modern agriculture. When the supplies failed to reach the newer construction zones, some investors began to question the value of more development and held back more funding. Loans for new development began to dry up, and calls were made for the paying of the short-term loans already made. Money became "tight," and banks began to require more from their customers in the form of down payments, shorter terms in loans or lines of credit and more collateral to secure the loans. Those who had speculated on a continuing boom in real estate and had purchased land on limited backing soon found themselves in a bind. Some of the larger

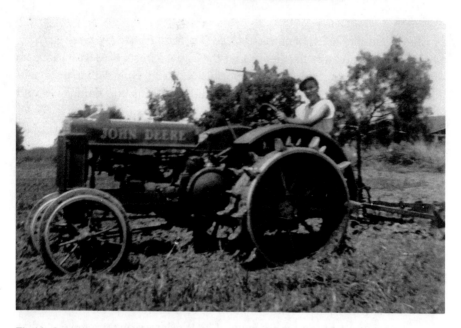

Florida farmers began to move from individual agricultural laborers to the use of tractors, trucks and other mechanized equipment in the late 1920s to compensate for the loss of African American field hands who were migrating to northern states. *Courtesy of the Manatee County Public Library System.*

farmers, feeling that there would be a continued growth in the demand for foodstuffs and cotton, bet on the future by investing in more machinery, land and crops.

Although some of the crops came in on time, the price was low and the loans high, thus creating a credit crunch for these entrepreneurs. The setup for a major fall had all the pieces in place by the end of 1926, and Florida entered a downturn that lasted until well into the New Deal years. The large number of bank failures was simply an indication of the troubles ahead. In the three years preceding the Wall Street crash, the state recorded 125 bank failures, most of which were state-chartered banks. When the banks slammed their doors shut, these closures amounted to nearly $105 million in deposits lost to customers. In those same three years, the state lost nearly two-thirds of its banking assets. Many people began asking how this could have happened and soon found their answers in the scandals of the banking system and the politicians who frequently benefited from their generosity.

Raymond Vickers, a seasoned veteran of Florida politics regarding the comptroller general's office, discovered many problems when researching his book, *Panic in Paradise: Florida's Banking Crash of 1926*, not the least of which was the fact that until he challenged that officer in the early 1990s, the records of the 1920s were still closed to researchers. What Vickers found was a web of interconnecting bankers, speculators and politicians who constantly covered up for each other until the game became too big for any of them. One of the many examples discovered by Vickers involved the connections between Comptroller Ernest Amos, W.D. Manley and J.R. Anthony, who was speaker pro tempore in 1925 and Senate president in 1929. The partnership of Manley and Anthony centered on the banking concerns in Jacksonville and Anthony becoming president of the Florida Bankers Association—a position that gave him power to appoint others to the group, including Forrest Lake, a state representative and president of the Seminole County Bank; Louis Bize, president and sometime confidant of Tampa power-broker Peter O. Knight; and J.H. Therrell of the Commercial Bank of Ocala. This group of bankers and politicians was behind the constitutional amendments that banned the income tax and inheritance taxes in Florida. All claimed to be following the lead of Secretary of the Treasury Andrew Mellon, who firmly believed that taxes inhibited investment. With Amos as comptroller and Hardee (and later Martin) as governors, they had little trouble getting the message out. What was not disclosed were their close interrelationships and business dealings, many of which bordered on out-and-out corruption.

As the downturn began, some people started asking questions as to the nature of the government regulation of the banking industry. Some of the largest newspapers began running stories stating that those who questioned the system knew little of it and were simply spreading panic among the general populace. One of the more outspoken newspapers was the *Tampa Morning Tribune*, which just happened to be run by Louis Bize, who also served as president of a bank, was formerly president of the Florida Bankers Association and was a partner in the Florida Title Insurance Company of Miami. Bize, to escape more scrutiny, sold the newspaper in 1927 to cover some debts of the Citizens Bank and Trust Company. The new owners did not play ball in the same court and published the news as it happened. When the panic hit the headlines in 1929, there was a run on the Citizens Bank and Trust Company, which quickly failed as the comptroller's office allowed it to stay open even though it was insolvent. Because of the bank secrecy laws in operation at the time, Bize and cohorts continued to abuse the establishment for an additional three years. In the end, the depositors were able to get only twenty-five cents on the dollar a decade later.

The spate of bank failures, most of which were state-chartered banks, and the growing suspicion that there was a cabal running the banking industry in Florida led to further distrust of the political system that allowed these things to happen. The general populace had only to look at the developers and "speculators" to see some of the causes of the economic downturn. The fact that most of them were "community leaders" and backers of the local politicians did little to allay the public's growing distrust. As the boom continued, many of the cities and towns expanded their infrastructures to cover the new subdivisions and developments. Roads, sewerage systems, water facilities and other municipal improvements were heavily invested in by the governing entities, and almost all issued bonds to cover the costs. When the downturn came and the developments were abandoned, the cities, counties and towns that had issued the bonds were stuck with the costs of paying them off. The total debt represented by these bonds was approximately $825 million, and few municipalities had the resources to pay them off. With Florida's highly restricted tax system, the options were few, and many of these governing bodies had to forfeit on the bonds, which destroyed their future credit ratings. The banks, which had issued or brokered the bonds for these entities, also lost heavily, contributing to the general loss of faith in the Florida banking system.

When John Martin left the governor's office, the state was deeply mired in the depression with little immediate hope of getting out. The devastation of the hurricane was soon compounded by the emergence of the Mediterranean fruit fly, which caused hundreds of citrus growers to destroy thousands of bearing trees in order to eradicate the pest. The large area covered by this infestation amounted to nearly 38 percent of the state's landmass. The production of citrus fell drastically for the growing season of 1929–1930, but because the growers, the state and the federal government acted with alacrity (spending almost $7 million in the process), the setback was confined to just those two seasons. The eradication program also temporarily employed nearly twenty thousand low-skilled workers, thus saving many from even more dire conditions. As historian James W. Dunn wrote, "The demise of the boom followed by natural disasters and the national depression combined to give Florida the highest unemployment rate in the Southeastern United States by 1930." Into this situation walked Florida's new governor, Doyle Carlton.

Doyle E. Carlton came into office after the very hotly contested elections of 1928 in which Florida gave the majority of its votes to the Republican presidential candidate, Herbert Hoover. This was the first time since Reconstruction that Florida had voted outside of the "solid South" Democratic tradition. The 1928 election saw the Democratic Party put up

Al Smith, a New York Catholic, as its candidate for president. This proved to be fodder for every anti-Catholic faction known to America, including former Florida governor Sidney J. Catts. Smith was not only a Catholic from New York, but he also favored the repeal of Prohibition, a highly unpopular stance with the Southern Baptists and Methodists who had worked so hard for its implementation. The Democrats were fractionalized by the national candidate, and many avoided discussing Smith's status as the party standard-bearer. One who did not shy away was Senator Duncan U. Fletcher. For his party loyalty he was known from that day forward as "Mr. Democrat" in Florida. Another newer face in the leadership of the party was a young Tallahassee-based attorney named Claude Pepper. Both men realized that the party would have to change to meet the emergencies of the present and that the party would have to take a different approach to the role of government in the future. Old-line Democrats, such as Carlton, Knight, Trammell and others, would have to adjust to the changes or be left out. Thus, in choosing Carlton, the fractionalized Democratic Party had taken a relatively safe road in the election for governor. It also assured itself that its powerful supporters would not be offended by some radical ideas that were beginning to be heard across the land. But this was not the wave of the future.

As a former state senator from Tampa, Carlton had close ties to Bize, Knight and the Anthony brothers. His philosophy of government reflected many of the ideas of the conservative faction of the Democrat Party. He campaigned for the conservative approach to government and the state's economic problems. He firmly believed that the depression being experienced by his fellow citizens was part of the regular cycle of business and that we had survived all in the past and this would be little different. Carlton also blamed the anarchists, communists and other dissenters for making the depression out to be worse than it actually was. Of course the new governor was for economizing in government (as if he had a choice) and was totally against any new taxes. He was totally opposed to the imposition of a sales tax and fervently against legalizing pari-mutuel betting. Along with others of the same persuasion, he blamed the infestation of the Mediterranean fruit fly for the demise of the banking structure. In this rather specious claim he echoed his friend Louis Bize, who blamed the invader for the failure of ten of his banks. However, as Raymond Vickers has pointed out, "Carlton…could not afford to discuss the real reasons for the disaster because he and his entities owed $218,578 in forty-three loans to the Citizens Bank and Trust Company at the time of its collapse." Even if Vickers's charges are exaggerated, the built-in philosophy of doing nothing of substance because everything would run its natural course did not bode well for the state financially or otherwise.

The 1929 session of the legislature produced very little in the way of innovative tax solutions to the financial problems of the state and local governments. Knowing that little could be expected from Washington in the way of aid, the state had to rely on its own resources, and they were dwindling almost daily. The major positive piece of legislation was the application of three cents of the five-cent gas tax to the relief of local governments for the liquidation of their bonded debts and the operation of the public schools. There was no move in the legislature to provide relief for the unemployed and needy. According to William J. Dunn's "The New Deal and Florida Politics," the most isolated Floridians, those in the hinterlands of northern Florida, were the ones in the most need. Their world, that of single-crop farming, tenant farming or sharecropping, was dying out. The gradual introduction of machines, primarily the tractor, reduced the need for unskilled manual labor, which was most demanded by the old cotton system. The lack of transportation facilities in the region, the exhaustion of the soil and the credit crunch on landowners made wage labor more attractive to the landowners and added to the unemployment rolls. Such jobs were minimum skill level jobs (hoeing, weeding and picking), and the changing economy of farming made these laborers into "hard-corps" unemployables. Their lot was not greatly improved by the later New Deal programs. What little schooling that was offered to these scattered, isolated families was of the old one-room schoolhouse in the woods. Low-tech vocational training, sewing room skills and home economics would not make them any more employable in the future, even if such classes were offered to them in convenient locations. These people seldom entered the minds of the lawmakers or their backers.

Carlton's second legislative session, that of 1931, was also challenged by the governor to be innovative in the face of the funding crisis. He asked for special consideration for the funding of education in general, the hospital for the insane, the courts system and other required governmental functions. The governor also promised to do his part in paring down the government's size while maintaining needed services, holding state employee salaries steady and scaling down certain departments to meet the contingencies. The legislature, for its part, began the session embroiled in debates over the proper uses of the gas tax and the legalization of pari-mutuel betting. At the end of the sixty-day session, no major decisions had been made regarding school funding, the allocation of the gas tax or any other significant measure. Carlton, frustrated by this inaction and petty squabbling, called two extra

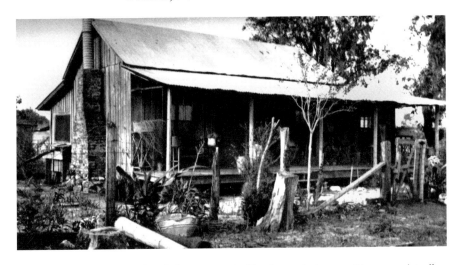

Small farmers trying to make a living on marginal lands saw their annual incomes virtually disappear by 1930. Sharecroppers and tenant farmers operated in an even more precarious economy as large landowners began to reduce the number of acres in cultivation. This is a picture of a small farmer's house in Hernando County in the early 1930s. *Courtesy of the Wynne Collection.*

sessions and literally forced the legislature to make decisions. The state now paid for 75 percent of the costs of the schools from general revenues, with the local counties picking up the remainder. The gas tax was diverted to the counties for debt reduction and road construction. The new tax passed to help support the increase in educational funding came with the fees levied on automobile license tags. In the end of this session, Carlton's final legislative stand, the state had avoided bankruptcy and saved its credit, but it did precious little else to end the woes of the state.

One final comment on the Carlton era came from Vickers when he noted that the 1931 session began the downfall of Carlton's old friend, Comptroller Ernest Amos. Carlton's Tampa backers and friends were intimates of Amos and supported his lack of enforcement of state banking laws. Audits showed that there was malfeasance during Amos's tenure and that many of the governor's friends were beneficiaries of his lax enforcement. The leader of the attack on Amos was J. Tom Watson, an attorney who formed the Tampa-based Bank Depositors Protective Association. One of his first actions in getting Amos removed was to get C.L. Knight removed as the receiver for the Citizens Bank, of which he happened to be a large stockholder and director. This obvious conflict of interest made for some rather interesting comments from the opposition. The governor was also involved with forestalling an attempt, or so it seemed to Peter O. Knight and others, by Alfred I. du Pont to take over the banking interests centered on the Citizens Bank group. Knight and others worked against any legislation that would allow the Jacksonville du Pont interests (headed by the ambitious Ed Ball) from gaining a foothold in Tampa. Watson and his group had no interest in Ball's expansion but did demand that Amos be impeached for protecting the ownership and not the depositors in the Citizens Bank and related institutions. The 1931 session did not impeach the comptroller, but the publicity brought about his defeat at the hands of J.M. Lee, and it left many questions regarding Carlton's behavior on behalf of his friends.

The perceived corruption of the highest officeholders and the worsening Depression made the 1932 election a real turning point for Floridians. New York governor Franklin D. Roosevelt had already begun to plow the fertile fields of Florida politics even before the results of the 1928 election were in the record books. The New York governor was quite familiar with Florida, having taken many fishing trips to the state in the mid-1920s until a hurricane put his houseboat, the *Lorooco*, in the trees near downtown Fort Lauderdale. On his last voyage in 1926, FDR told his mother of his purchase of the property in Warm Springs, Georgia, with the hope that she would help make it handicap accessible. FDR had many new ideas about governing the nation and was to some extent experimenting with them as governor of New York. Many of his economic advisers cut their political teeth while serving in his administration. The impact of the depressed economy made many people willing to try something new, even if it did not work. The Hoover approach to laissez-faire economics as a cure for the Depression simply was not working, and people were suffering without jobs, money, property or hope. The only really meaningful program introduced by the Hoover administration was the Reconstruction Finance Corporation (RFC), which was an extension of the War Finance Corporation (WFC) left over from the First World War and headed by the talented banker Eugene Meyer. The sale and financing of Liberty Bonds and the extension of export credits were the bread and butter of this organization. Hoover opposed the extension of the WFC and the creation of the RFC, but despite opposition from the president and Secretary of the Treasury Andrew Mellon, the emergency was simply too large to submit to the voluntary solutions favored by the president, and Congress enacted the bill to create the RFC. Even though the RFC was not really a new agency, it was successful in getting over $55 million in loans out to businesses greatly in need of cash. The key combination in getting Hoover to approve this important act was Meyer and the Democratic leader in the senate, Joseph T. Robinson. The success of the RFC set the stage for a number of changes put forth in the "Hundred Days" by FDR.

The voters in Florida were also tired of hearing about business cycles, laissez-faire economics and "business man's government," and they demanded change. By 1932, nearly a quarter of all Floridians were on some kind of relief, and what they needed was work and steady income. The RFC provided some relief loans and funds (nearly $2 million worth), but Governor Carlton had only asked for $500,000, just to get things going again. With an economy stretched to the limit, major natural disasters, the fruit fly, the boll weevil and the national Depression, Floridians needed much more than reassurances that business would naturally turn around. With a state-level income of $517 per capita, compared to the national average of $698, Florida was behind the rest of the nation even at the beginning of the Carlton era. Yet, dismal as these figures were, Florida still had a higher per capita personal income than any other former Confederate state. But as economist William B. Stronge warned, per capita income figures were not the best measure of Florida's true condition since so many of the transfer, interest and dividends payments did not remain in the state but were held by part-time residents and investors from out of state. By 1930, Floridians in the mining, forestry, fishing and agriculture sectors of the economy found themselves facing major job losses. In 1900, these industries employed 52 percent of Florida's labor force, but by 1930 that number had dropped to 25 percent. Because so many of these industries employed less skilled workers, the impact on the overall economy was larger than anticipated. Much more time, money and effort would have to be put into making these segments more marketable in the future, and money was something Florida did not have. Little wonder that Florida voters demanded change—and fast!

The Florida election of 1932 featured two former governors, Martin and Hardee, who ran on their past performances. Tampa attorney J. Tom Watson and the then-president of the Florida Chamber of Commerce, David Sholtz of Daytona Beach, were also considered possibilities. Martin was considered the front-runner in the beginning, since Hardee was not the campaigner he once was and times had drastically changed. Running on his record, Hardee's candidacy meant simply the same old thing, and that pleased fewer and fewer voters as the campaign wore on to a climax in the first primary. (Florida had a dual primary system then.)

Sholtz was the outsider from the beginning. He was born in Brooklyn, New York, in 1891. He was the son of a Russian immigrant, Yale educated and a Stetson Law School graduate. Possessing a dynamic personality, he

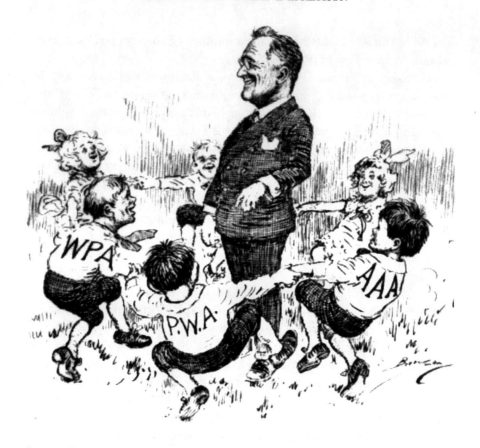

Governor David P. Sholtz was a firm believer in the ideas of Franklin Delano Roosevelt and correctly understood that the myriad agencies FDR created when he assumed the presidency in 1933 would benefit every Floridian. *Courtesy of Arva Parks McCabe.*

exuded optimism that he could make things better, and he was trusted by the business community in the Sunshine State. Sholtz was a hard campaigner and enjoyed meeting the voters face to face and interacting with them. He had served only one term in the legislature and had managed to invite the wrath of the Volusia "Courthouse Gang" when he did not embrace their values of cronyism and favoritism. Sholtz also served in the military during World War I and was commissioned an ensign in the navy (serving on the censorship board at Key West and Havana, Cuba). He surprised old-time political pundits when he made the second primary and became the only remaining opponent to John Martin. In the final runoff, the personable, energetic Sholtz visited nearly every major voting area in the state, and the result was the largest margin of victory ever recorded in the history of the state. In the general election, against real estate developer W.J. Howey of the Republican Party, the margin was nearly two to one in Sholtz's favor.

Running as the Democratic candidate, Sholtz made no secret of his support for the new programs promised by FDR. As historian Merlin Cox noted in his article on Sholtz, the governor promised to follow the lead of the Democratic presidential candidate and to take a new approach to Florida's financial woes and unemployment. Roosevelt won an overwhelming victory in Florida, and Sholtz, in his first address to the legislature, reiterated his support for FDR: "President Roosevelt has boldly shown the way to the nation and Congress has worked with him for the solution of the national problems. I can only ask that you, within all constitutional grounds, work with me in finding the solution of our state problem." He then proposed to reduce the cost of the license tags to a more reasonable rate, create a department of conservation for the state and called for the restructuring of the finances for public schools. His biggest obstacle, surprisingly, was the question of free textbooks for public school students, which some legislators considered "socialistic." With much cajoling and horse-trading, and with his winning personality in full force, Sholtz was able to persuade the reluctant legislators that this was best for the children—and in the end he triumphed. He also started an investigation into the condition of the road camps, many of which lacked plumbing and hot water. Sholtz noted that the cattle on Florida's ranches often received better care than the inmates, many of whom were serving minor sentences. Most importantly, his staunch support of Roosevelt put the state in line for more favorable treatment than others that were more critical of the new growth of the federal government. Sholtz's final promise to the legislature and the people of Florida was to work toward eliminating the deficit in the state budget. In 1933, that deficit stood at $2,124,000, but with hard work and increased income from licenses, the gas tax and other sources, the deficit became a surplus of $591,000 by June 30, 1934.

The question of repealing Prohibition in Florida was decided long before people went to the polls. A *Literary Digest* poll taken just prior to the election showed Florida's voters were overwhelmingly in favor of the repeal. The tough stance of Congresswoman Ruth Bryan Owens against repeal cost her her seat in Congress. The futility of enforcement and the costs (especially in potential tax dollars) to the state in lost revenue were the deciding factors. The public sentiment for repeal was overwhelming. The 1933 legislature, with the new governor's approval, put a constitutional amendment that would end Prohibition on the next general election ballot.

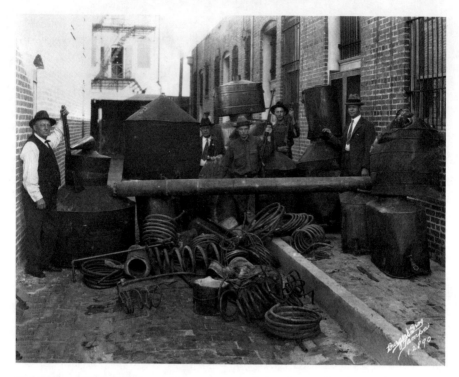

Prohibition, a World War I war measure, was repealed in the early 1930s in the Sunshine State, an action that closely followed the repeal of the measure at the national level. *Courtesy of the Burgert Brothers Collection, Tampa Public Library.*

Governor Sholtz faced an enormous task in reforming Florida's antiquated government. Restructuring the tax system was one of his top priorities, and he plunged immediately into the task of finding solutions to this problem. Aided by State Senator Spessard Holland and Representative S. Pierre Robineau in the House, Sholtz tried to get a total overhaul of the system through the 1933 legislature. The main thrust of his proposed overhaul was a bill to create a tax commission board composed of the governor, comptroller and state treasurer. The bill would authorize the board to put counties and municipalities that had defaulted on their debts into receivership so the state could make proper adjustments to the debts and pay them off. It also proposed giving the commission a line item veto over future expenses by the indebted entities. This part of the proposed law was vehemently opposed by the Florida League of Municipalities and the bondholders' lobbyists. The Speaker of the House, Peter Tomasello, also served as the consultant for the League of Municipalities and mobilized his supporters in the House against it. Representative Robineau, who was leading the fight for the bill in the House, was not able to overcome the opposition of the Speaker and his political friends. In the end, the Speaker's vote broke the tie and the reform bill died for that session. The governor had lost the battle, but the war was just beginning. The fight for the passage of the bill was close in the Senate, but Senator Holland exercised his considerable influence to persuade other senators, and it passed in that body.

The ambitious governor also tried to push through an expanded workman's compensation law for Florida's laborers. This reform was a holdover from the earlier Progressive Era and one that was opposed throughout the agricultural South, not just Florida. The main argument against the adoption of this plan was the South's "peculiar situation," the predominance of agriculture as the main industry of the region, which would cost too much for farmers and planters to pay. New York was the first state to adopt this reform in 1910, and by 1934, forty-five states had put some form of workman's compensation law into effect. Florida was not one of the states to have such a law on the books.

The basic idea behind such a law was that employers would be held liable for injuries suffered by workers on the job—no matter what the cause of the injury—within specified limits. Workers would gain assurances that they would, indeed, be properly compensated for a work-related injury. Insurance companies, which had originally opposed such legislation but threw their support to Sholtz's proposed law, would gain from the fact that employers would be required to carry insurance on all of their workers, thus adding the revenues from new policies to their coffers. In addition, the restrictions placed on awards limited their liabilities.

The insurance industry's biggest fear was that states would set up competing insurance programs, thus depriving investors of a chance for more profits. The compromises represented by most state-run workman's compensation plans all had elements that benefited both workers and investors. In Florida, however, the legislature "fiddled while Rome burned." In the 1933 session, the bill got "lost in the shuffle" during extended arguments over the distribution of a new tax on legalized beer. The session ended without any action on this popular piece of legislation. However, Sholtz was not to be outdone, and a bill was reintroduced in the 1935 session that did pass, leaving Arkansas and Mississippi as the only states without such a law. Governor Sholtz's continuous pressure, along with laborers and other groups that stood to benefit by its passage, finally overcame the legislature's reluctance to act, but only after agricultural workers were exempted from mandatory coverage.

Florida's educational system was supported by a hodgepodge of local and state funding in the early 1930s. Little direction and oversight to the operations of schools was given, except at the local level, and this was where Sholtz and political leaders placed the blame for the system's pathetic performances. Sholtz asked the legislature for, and got, a State Board of Control to oversee the revamping of Florida's educational system, which would create a unified, state-run system with uniform programs throughout the state. This was a very important step forward, since most migration in Florida took place from county to county rather than state to state. Much of this in-migration took place from rural areas to cities in an attempt to find employment and more flexible relief programs. This was a national trend and was not just indigenous to Florida.

Governor Sholtz had gotten his free textbook legislation passed but immediately faced another problem in funding a statewide educational system and allocation of tax monies to county districts. Sholtz wanted to equalize funding between all counties and to make the assessments of property taxes for schools more equitable. As an opponent of the sales tax, which he considered too regressive, he thought the answer would be a more equitable distribution of the gas tax funds and that license tag fees would be a move in the right direction. He also wanted control over the minimum salary level for teachers, an increase in teacher pay and a state program to administer the school funds generally. The governor's plan was opposed by the Florida Education Association and most local school boards, which feared state interference in what they believed was a local responsibility. Sholtz in turn blamed the economic predicament of the local schools on poor management at the county level. In the end, Sholtz got some of his reforms—like the statewide school board and redistribution of the taxes on gas and license fees—but he did not get all that he wanted. Again, Sholtz accepted what he could get, choosing compromise with his opponents on some issues but reforming the educational system nevertheless.

Sholtz had promised voters to make government more efficient, and upon entering office, he immediately asked for the resignation of most appointed officials still in office from the Carlton regime. He then removed all the relatives of department heads who occupied a number of positions in state agencies. Nepotism had always been the bane of state government, but Sholtz would have none of it. Since he was considered a political outsider, he carried none of the political baggage of a Martin, Hardee or Carlton. As the natural father of only one child (he and wife Alice did adopt two daughters, and one orphan boy lived with the family during these years, although he was not officially adopted), maybe he did not see any reason for appointing his relatives to jobs in Florida's government. As an opponent of the old "Courthouse Gang" in Volusia County, he had little use for the family networks that dominated local governments. As a successful businessman and head of the Chamber of Commerce, he probably also realized that hiring your mother-in-law as a shop foreman might not be the best way to run a business efficiently. His trimming of the staffs of many departments and bureaus was met with approval from most voters.

A proposed constitutional amendment to raise the homestead exemption for Floridians provoked heated debates among politicians, although Sholtz managed to avoid having to take a side on the matter. Establishing a $5,000 exemption for the principal residence of each citizen, the measure was designed as a way to relieve homeowners and small farmers from some of the tax burden that many felt hindered growth. As a small stimulus package, it appealed to the real estate establishment and many persons in banking and investing. The proposed exemption was the first of its kind in the nation, and as James W. Dunn points out, it "gave Florida national prominence as a laboratory for modern tax experiments." Some of the proposed amendment's supporters also saw it as a means to begin the major tax reform that Florida needed. Although proponents expected some support from Sholtz and, to a lesser extent, from the president, neither one spoke out on the issue in public. Neither man wanted to alienate potential voters in the upcoming 1936 presidential race or disturb some of the opponents who were in office in the 1935 legislative session. The leader of the exemption forces was Senator (later Senate President) William C. Hodges. When the amendment passed by a three-to-one margin, he was seen by many as the most powerful man in Florida politics. Luckily for Sholtz, he had cultivated a good relationship with Hodges, and as the latter was a political realist, each man understood the stance of the other relative to the amendment. Sholtz expected the exemption to cost the state nearly $1 million in revenue, but he was willing to search for new sources to offset the loss.

For Florida, the 1935 legislative session was one of the most significant sessions in the twentieth century. Sholtz, who had received encouragement for his reforms from the White House, knew things had to change—and soon. Many Floridians, some already on the brink of starvation, desperately needed help, and the old ways of doing things by state government were inadequate to deal with the problems. For all of their generosity and caring, private relief agencies and churches simply could not handle the level of need, so aggressive state action was needed. Sholtz made a personal commitment that he would institute what amounted to a mini–New Deal for Florida and follow the president's lead in developing relief programs for the unemployed. Although Peter O. Knight and other leading political figures counseled otherwise, Sholtz saw that the suffering and despair many citizens faced had to be relieved. Inaction, he felt, was tantamount to murder, but he knew it would not be easy to change the minds of the wealthy and privileged members of Florida's upper classes.

Some of the well-to-do farmers in the Panhandle and elsewhere in the state had some "interesting experiences" with the Agricultural Adjustment Act (AAA), a New Deal effort to curtail crop production, and were not favorably impressed. Although the AAA allowed them to divest themselves of the responsibility of providing for their former tenants and sharecroppers, while taking payments to not grow certain crops like cotton and tobacco, these farmers were opposed to any program that would weaken their control over local laborers. Stipulations in the AAA program regarding payments to tenants, in particular, were ignored, and the landowners simply pocketed the money and forced their former employees to become wage laborers. Unfortunately, most of them had few marketable skills for the new industrial age that was rapidly growing everywhere. Retraining workers who could not read or write would take time and money, and some landowners were unwilling to see either spent on these landless, mostly African American people. Many of these unfortunates migrated to Florida's growing cities in search of work and education. While some were lucky and found both, many became part of the "hardcore" unemployed. Government programs for relief were frowned upon by conservative elements in the state's Democratic Party, but Sholtz was willing to buck the opposition of this group and supported the use of New Deal programs for the benefit of Floridians in general.

Even before the beginning of the 1935 session, Governor Sholtz had indicated his desire to follow the president's lead. At the beginning of the session, he addressed the legislature and noted that the New Deal had made available millions of dollars for emergency relief that was desperately needed by Floridians who were now unemployed through no fault of their own. He also reminded political supporters and opponents of the unusual degree of cooperation between the federal government and the State of Florida, and he indicated he was not willing to give up this cooperation, which he argued would be an act of bad faith. Sholtz also stated that he would continue to balance the budget in order to protect the state's reputation as a fiscally conservative state. The governor hit upon a popular theme in his address, and it was one he would continue to expand upon throughout the session.

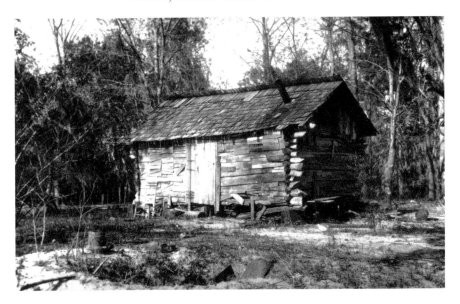

A sharecropper's cabin in rural Hernando County. As more sharecroppers and tenant farmers left rural areas and headed to cities and towns to look for work, cabins like these were abandoned and left to the elements. *Courtesy of the Wynne Collection.*

When the session opened, Governor Sholtz asked legislators for what appeared to be a balanced budget, with increased funding for schools, additional funding for the state mental hospital and expansion of the prison system. At this point in time, Florida had not supplied one dollar in matching funds for the federal relief it had received. One of the major bottlenecks for the governor was the lack of funds generated by the taxes on beer and wine sales, because no state agency existed to enforce the rules and oversee the collection of the taxes. The same problem existed for pari-mutuel betting. Sholtz proposed the creation of a state liquor control board and a racing commission to enforce the taxes and assure the public of fairness in the application of the tax code. Neither a racing commission nor a liquor control board had been included in the authorizing legislation, whether by design or faulty staff work, and this meant that no effective enforcement of the tax laws had been possible. Because the federal government had threatened to withhold money if the schools were not properly funded, the state was forced into creating agencies that would ensure compliance.

What followed next was a blizzard of new legislation—so many new bills that legislators, not used to such a rapid pace of activity, were frequently confused. Following our "wise president's example," Florida legislators launched a mini–New Deal and passed some of the most important legislation in the state's history. The conservatives in the party, led by party chairman James Hodges, were appalled at the prospect of such rapid change and set up opposition headquarters in Tallahassee's Floridian Hotel to try to stem the barrage of new laws. This effort was futile, however, in the face of the overwhelming needs of Floridians and the requirements of federal programs. One of the first bills to pass in the session called for a moratorium on public indebtedness. Opponents filed for an injunction in federal court to stop the application of the law, and the moratorium was found to be in violation of the Fourteenth Amendment of the United States Constitution. Sholtz, when the final bill reached his desk, was forced to veto the legislation under the threat of federal action by the Public Works Administration to curtail grants and loans to the state under its various programs. A fight over sales tax provoked a major fight between the governor and legislators, but it ended when Sholtz introduced a bill that would exempt transactions in bonds, insurance or other forms of indebtedness.

The expansion of state government now began in earnest with the creation of a large number of agencies to oversee or create new entities. The State Liquor Control Board was created and empowered to control licenses, regulate and tax the sale of alcohol and collect all taxes due. The biggest opposition to this came from Senator Holland, not because of the taxing powers but because he opposed the "State of Florida getting into the liquor business." This act was quickly followed by the creation of the State Employment Board, the State Tuberculosis Board and the Citrus Commission. As if these were not enough new agencies, the governor and legislature also created a State Planning Board (today's Department of Management Services), the Florida Game and Fresh Water Fish Commission (Florida Wildlife Commission), the State Park Service (now part of the Department of Environmental Protection) and the Everglades Park Commission. The Everglades Park Commission was authorized to purchase properties needed for the park and to transfer state lands acquired under the Everglades Patent (No. 137) to the federal government. The State Board of Forestry (now the Division of Forestry under the Department of Agriculture) was also established. Some political observers alleged that this was set up to protect and preserve the Alfred du Pont investments in north Florida timberlands (St. Joe Paper Company today), but this is highly debatable since the large number of state forests created at the time are located throughout the state and not just in northern Florida. The main functions of this agency were fire protection, tree replacement (in overharvested areas) and forest management. In cooperation with the Civilian Conservation Corps (CCC) and the Works Progress Administration (WPA), this agency grew into one of the most important relief agencies in the state. The State Park Service also benefited greatly from the work of the CCC and WPA from the donations of thousands of acres of relatively virgin lands by private individuals. The addition of the state parks added even more Florida tourist destinations.

Although many opposed the creation of the workman's compensation legislation, Florida quickly utilized its workings for the benefit of all injured workers. The state quickly set up the Florida Industrial Commission to administer the legislation. The name of the commission indicated that the application of compensation laws did not include agricultural workers or workers in service industries.

A state relief act was approved that provided financial and psychological assistance to Florida's older workers. Pushed by the Florida Association for Social Legislation and its president, Elizabeth Cooley, Florida quickly organized the State Welfare Board, which took over the social work tasks originally administered under the Federal Emergency Relief Administration (FERA). Set up under the Social Welfare Act, the Welfare Board not only administered the funding for the elderly but also oversaw the spending for aid to dependent children and to those with severe disabilities, including the blind. A constitutional amendment passed later in 1935 provided for state matching funds for old age assistance.

Other notable legislation passed by the 1935 session includes the Uniform Mechanics Lien Act, which protected property and moveable goods from foreclosure on past debts. It also passed a chain store tax that was meant to raise revenue and protect local stores from unfair competition of the mass marketing chain stores. It also faced the normally daunting task of creating a new congressional district, a clear indication of the numbers of people Florida was gaining in population even in the midst of a national depression. An act to aid in judicial recruiting also passed during the session. With an ever-increasing population and a likely increase in the crime rate, legislators felt there was a need to recruit and train future judges and law enforcement officers. The 1935 legislative session was a whirlwind of activity and positive achievements. Cooperation among the governor, Senator Hodges and others paved the way for a new and brighter future for Florida, and the impact of their work is still felt today.

Sholtz spent his remaining time in office lobbying Washington for more money and changes in programs that would help Florida. He was active in trying to get more Floridians employed but had the problem of many governors of other states—more job seekers than jobs. He was very proud of his service to Florida, but as most decisive politicians do, he made his share of enemies while in office. Some opponents accused him of being too tight with the pari-mutuel industry, and others whispered that he was "on the take," although no one ever proved these allegations. Most of the conservatives in the Democratic Party were opposed to the reform programs that were passed during his administration. Yet when he left office, he could boast he had kept his promise to Floridians and balanced the budget every year, even leaving his successor a small surplus. But like other politicians in Florida's past, he could not parlay his successes as governor into higher office. When he ran for the United States Senate in 1938, he was defeated by another proponent of the New Deal, Claude Pepper, who many felt had been cheated out of the office in 1934. After this defeat, Sholtz went back to Daytona Beach and split his time between Florida and the mountains of North Carolina with his beloved "Allie." After an automobile accident in 1952, David Sholtz suffered a heart attack and died. He is buried in the Cedar Hill Cemetery in Daytona Beach.

Chapter 4

THE NEW DEAL
UNDER ATTACK IN THE
SUNSHINE STATE

Even though Florida spends millions of dollars annually to advertise its attributes
and encourage out-of-state people to come here and spend their money, Floridians
resent outsiders on public payrolls.
—*Jack Horne, CCC selection agent in Florida*

David Sholtz's successor in office was Fred P. Cone of Columbia County, whose major claim to fame prior to his running for public office was shooting a former Yankee who was about to be appointed as the new postmaster in White Springs. After attending the Jasper Normal College, Cone matriculated to the Florida Agricultural College in Lake City (later moved to Gainesville as the University of Florida). After briefly studying law, he passed his bar examination and was admitted to practice in 1892. He soon turned to banking in the small county seat of Lake City, where he made a reputation for himself as a conservative, Old South kind of banker, who was often difficult to deal with but always fair with his clients. His father, a major influence in his life, had been a state senator in the antebellum period, and Cone wished to emulate that feat. In 1907, Cone got his wish and was elected to the Florida Senate, and in 1911, was elected president of that body. According to historian David Nelson, Cone's one major bill during these early years provided for a pension for Confederate veterans. Although this appears trivial by today's standards, this was a major triumph for the veterans and their heirs, who had sought pensions for over four decades. For many Floridians, this assured Cone a place in their hearts and reminded them of his southern roots, an important credential for Florida office seekers in those days.

Cone was always a faithful Democrat and served as a delegate to three national conventions. During his last convention, 1928, he made a name for himself by opposing and then refusing to vote for Al Smith as the party's presidential nominee. For the first time, he became known to voters outside Columbia County. His brief moment of fame was to serve him well in the gubernatorial election of 1936, when fourteen candidates put themselves into the race. Cone had a solid base in northern Florida, and his old-style campaign went over well with voters who had been skeptical of the suave, sophisticated Sholtz. The *Ocala Banner* referred to Cone as "a cracker from head to toe," and that he was, unashamedly. Other than being an opponent of the programs of the outgoing Sholtz, he offered very little that was new or even in agreement with many New Deal programs. Yet, he portrayed himself as a loyal Democrat, but one who would insist upon a balanced budget, small government and no new taxes. He also took a shot at the New Deal's higher wage standards, especially for the large number of out-of-state government workers. What he wanted, he declared, was "Florida labor at living wages for all public works." Although he did not state it boldly, he also wanted the privilege of appointing as many government employees as possible, especially in the New Deal–sponsored agencies.

Senator Spessard Holland viewed Cone as a "very conservative and overly cautious small town banker." In an interview with historian James Dunn, Holland noted that Cone was old-fashioned in his thinking and obstinate and inflexible in dealing with those who opposed him. Although he loved his home state, Holland felt Cone was "simply too old to be governor." Too old or not, the Democratic voters of Florida put him into office to end the alleged corruption of the last years of the Sholtz administration. It must be assumed that those who supported his nomination did not consider the resumption of cronyism and nepotism "corrupt," and he made little secret of his desire to rid Florida of all "outside interference" brought about by the New Deal agencies.

Cone's inaugural address should have been ample warning of changes to come. He noted that after reading the budget report for 1937, he was not in agreement with it since it actually contained more than he thought was needed to run the state government. In his address, he called for a return to business principles in running the government and emphasized the need for smaller government to balance the budget, forgetting for the moment that

Sholtz had never run a deficit and left him with a small surplus. One of his main targets was the State Road Department, because much of the money spent by that agency was earmarked for projects in the southern parts of the state. He also advocated the consolidation and reductions in the size of state agencies, especially those employing out-of-state workers.

What made this difficult to understand was Cone's insistence that he was a loyal supporter of FDR and the New Deal. Perhaps his attitude stemmed from his old-fashioned "solid South" support of all Democrats, which was ironic coming from someone who refused to work for Al Smith in 1928. His backing of FDR's plan for "packing the Supreme Court of the United States" and advocacy of the Child Labor Law Amendment in Florida caused some confusion among his conservative backers, yet enough of his anti–New Deal philosophy came through his other actions to more than make up for these slight transgressions. He was also determined to keep his campaign promise to not interfere with the workings of the legislature, and in 1937, he offered no program proposals of his own. Cone made no attempt to form a solid block of support within the legislature, as Sholtz had done, but left the legislative body free to do as it pleased. As political columnist John Kilgore states, this "apparent lack of leadership…[was] due to the fact that there [was] no administration program and consequently no administration bloc behind it." As Dunn noted, the only legislation pushed by the new governor was the repeal of the act legalizing slot machines.

Cone also opposed the operations of the State Board of Social Welfare, which had been headquartered in Jacksonville after Harry Hopkins, who was in charge of FDR's social welfare programs, feared too much Tallahassee control might ensue during the Sholtz era. Little did Hopkins know of Cone's enmity toward outsider influence and the head of the FERA in Florida, Conrad Van Hyning. Van Hyning had garnered vast experiences operating social programs in New York and was one of several New Yorkers brought into New Deal agencies by Roosevelt. Surprisingly, it was David Sholtz who asked for Van Hyning to be appointed the FERA chief in Florida. When Van Hyning came to the state and took over as the Florida welfare commissioner, he found himself in charge of an agency with few, if any, trained staff with professional experience in administering programs that dealt with social welfare issues. He was forced by circumstances to find qualified help from the outside, thus setting himself up as a target for the incoming governor. Florida's CCC selecting agent, Jack Horne, commented on Cone's opposition: "Even though Florida spends millions of dollars annually to advertise its attributes and encourage out-of-state people to come here and spend their money, Floridians resent outsiders on public payrolls." In the eyes of Cone and his backers, these professionals were "foreigners" in the state.

When Van Hyning and his staff created a merit system for evaluating potential new hires—a move aimed at preventing patronage appointments—he ran afoul of Cone and his cronies, who were intent on doing away with this outsider-run board and replacing it with something more amenable to their way of doing things. In April 1937, Cone began the attack on the board by asking the legislature to investigate the agency for financial corruption. He then replaced State Auditor Bryan Willis with a friend, William Wainwright, who began his own investigation of the State Board of Social Welfare. Cone ordered background checks on the board's employees, which included looking into places of origins, salaries, family connections, whether or not they had the proper tags on their vehicles and whether or not they were Jewish. With the aid of State Senator William Mapoles of Crestview and State Representative Robert Sikes, he soon abolished the existing board, saw to it that Van Hyning was removed and made sure that the funding was too low to accomplish some of its tasks, including providing aid to dependent children and to the blind. This was hardly done in the spirit of cooperation with the Roosevelt administration in Washington, and it has been argued that Cone's actions set Florida back by many years in providing welfare services to those most in need. Eventually, the State Board of Social Welfare was abolished and replaced by the State Welfare Board, a move that opened this agency to widespread patronage and corruption.

Cone's penchant for placing friends in office, which included appointing his former law partner, Roy Chapman, to the State Supreme Court, disrupted the progressive reforms of the Sholtz years. He hired his brother, Branch (aka "the Joker"), as his executive secretary. Branch was known as his brother's "patronage chief" and often investigated potential employees for their political views and voting records. The governor even went so far as to veto legislation that enabled the state to participate in the unemployment compensation insurance program. He refused to approve any measure unless the agency guaranteed that administrative officials would be official residents of the state of Florida for at least five years and unless a cap on the wages of employees of the Compensation Board was put in place. In the end, he got his way.

One of the few bright spots of the Cone years was the repeal of the poll tax, which limited voting by poor whites and African Americans and had become part of the legacy of the post-Reconstruction era. The leader of the repeal was Senator Ernest L. Graham of Miami, who had to overcome some very powerful opposition from conservative white politicians. According to James Dunn, "The opposing forces were comprised, for the most part, of a coalition of South Florida politicians supported by the racing and gambling interests who had built up blocs of voters by paying poll taxes for them, and the school lobby, who feared the repeal would cut off poll tax revenue earmarked for school use." Florida's newest U.S. senator, Claude Pepper, took the side of those who wanted the tax repealed, primarily because he and his followers felt that it would expand the political base of politicians who supported New Deal legislation in Florida. By some shrewd maneuvering, Graham was able to get the repeal legislation admitted as a local bill, which made it non-controversial, and by appeasing the school lobby with an increase in their funding from the general revenue, Graham was able to neutralize their opposition. The race issue, which normally would have been in the forefront of this debate, was avoided by Graham's adroit political moves. Because this did not remove the restrictions on black voting in the Democratic primaries, it did not offend white politicians like those in Tampa's White Municipal Party.

The 1937 legislature also passed the Murphy Act, which transferred, at least temporarily, the title of thousands of parcels of land to the state for resale and reinstatement on local tax rolls. The legislature noted that the state already had a land agency, the Board of Trustees of the Internal Improvement Trust Fund (TIIF), and hoped that by having this agency resell the tax-delinquent land titles, the property would soon be purchased and the land restored to the local tax rolls. No one thought that the state would hold permanent title to these lands. In the course of administering this large land transaction, over 541,000 parcels were sent (or allegedly sent) to the state for resale. To handle this load, the budget for the TIIF was increased by only one full-time position and one half-time position. The duties of the new employees were to personally review and pass on the validity of these titles for purpose of resale. It was an impossible task for one and a half people to review and record over half a million parcels in the short time that the state held title. This act was repealed in the very next legislative session because of pressure from the local "Courthouse Gangs," whose incomes were diminished by the loss of control of such properties.

The 1937 legislative session was not a particularly active or progressive session, and little was accomplished to improve economic conditions in the state. At the urging of Governor Cone, legislators outlawed slot machines throughout the state and defeated efforts to reform laws governing the general sales tax, taxes on amusement parks and luxury taxes. The legislature refused to consider a repeal of the constitutional amendments banning income and inheritance taxes. It also refused to pass a measure to require the fencing of pastures for cattle or other livestock, which contributed to a growing number of deaths on Florida highways. On the whole, the 1937 session was a regressive attempt by Cone and his conservative supporters to repeal the reforms of the Sholtz administration and to restore Florida politics to the way they were before the New Deal. The obstructionist attitudes of the conservatives began to change when the federal government threatened to withhold some of the funding for the CCC and WPA projects in Florida, and, in the words of David Nelson, "many of Cone's supporters bolted."

Prior to the 1939 session, the State Budget Commission met to discuss the state's needs. The commission meetings, which were not attended by the Governor Cone because of illness, arrived at the conclusion that the previous two years had not produced enough revenue to continue to support the state programs already in existence. Incoming legislators were warned that there was a need for new sources of revenue or an increase in the current tax rates to cover the expected expenses. Cone was obstinate in his refusal to consider any such measures, and he was immediately challenged in this by the new Senate president, Senator J. Turner Butler. Butler argued that a tax increase was unavoidable and reminded Floridians of the increase in the state's population, which placed additional burdens on its agencies. In spite of the sharp downturn in the national economy in 1937–38, the Sunshine State had experienced growth in wealth and could now afford modest tax increases. The battle lines were drawn for a major battle over the budget, which was operating with a short-term deficit because of the inaction of the 1937 legislature and Cone's vetoes of tax measures. Luckily for the state's finances, wealthy philanthropist and landowner Alfred du Pont died in April 1939, and the state's share of his estate amounted to nearly $2 million. This unexpected income erased the deficit and allowed the 1939 session to start budgetary considerations without having to immediately find ways to fund overruns.

Although the 1939 legislature did little to alleviate the situation of no new tax monies or to pass any legislation that could be considered innovative, the session did see a proposed resolution submitted for consideration that augured well for the future. Two new legislators, LeRoy Collins of Tallahassee and Dan McCarty of Fort Pierce, teamed up to propose a general overhaul of the existing tax structure. Although the resolution went nowhere because of Cone's outspoken disapproval, it did introduce Floridians to two future governors. The only positive action of the legislature, if it can be called that, was that it overrode more gubernatorial vetoes than any other legislature in the state's history. One of the few important vetoes that the legislature could not overcome was that of the $3 million appropriation addition to the budget. Unfortunately, most of the overrides concerned local issues and nothing of statewide significance. Because of Cone's stubborn resistance to new taxes, the state ended the year with a deficit for the first time since 1932. Overall, the 1939 session was a dismal failure. When the next election cycle came around in 1940, Cone ran for the U.S. Senate—he finished fourth in a six-man race.

Florida was due for a change, and it refused to be goaded into electing another Fred Cone. Once again, the Democratic primary featured eleven candidates, but the front-runner this time was Spessard Holland of Polk County. Holland was an experienced politician and "a man of quality" who was admired by his contemporaries. With the death of former Senate President William Hodges, Holland was one of the few leaders whom politicians could rely on for good, sound conservative government; yet, he was not a conservative of the same stripe as Cone.

After attending the public schools in Polk County, Holland graduated from Emory College (now University) and then headed for the University of Florida in 1916. At the outbreak of the First World War, he volunteered for service and was commissioned a second lieutenant in the artillery and assigned to coastal defense sites. But he wanted more. A young man of action, Holland requested flying duty in France, which was granted, and, after a short training in the fledgling flight service, was assigned to the Twenty-Fourth Aero Squadron on the Meuse-Argonne, St. Michel and Lineville fronts. He received the Distinguished Service Cross and, after the war, returned to Florida to practice law in Bartow. His service as county prosecuting attorney and county judge earned him the respect of his peers and voters. In 1932, they sent him to Tallahassee as a state senator, where he served until he was elected governor in 1940. Under his leadership, and in cooperation with the United States government, the state began preparations for the coming war. He led the TIIF in leasing or donating lands for the many airfields, training grounds and bombing ranges throughout the state. Many of today's colleges and universities sit on the sites of these former training bases left over from World War II—they remain part of Governor Holland's legacy.

Chapter 5

BISCUIT AND 'TATER TIME

None of us had anything to speak of, but we all had fun because it was the same for everyone back then.
—*Ruby Long Chavous,* Gainesville Sun, *July 10, 2009*

The end of the Florida land boom of the 1920s impacted everyone in the state, and towns that had appeared overnight soon either went back to the wilderness or became memories of subdivisions never completed. Cities and towns throughout Florida suffered from what they saw as a great crash, nearly three years before the Wall Street debacle. What happened in little Delray Beach may have been typical. As Cecil and Margoann Farrar described it, "It was in the winter of 1925–26 that a sense of warning fell over the town, like a creeping paralysis. Then, almost before anyone could grasp the truth, the boom was over." In addition to the often-described freight congestion along the railroads and the embargoes placed on incoming construction materials, the Farrars take note of another cause: "Perhaps the greatest cause of the real estate debacle was that the boom had no basis in reality. Prosperity was manufactured, fed by the contagious enthusiasm of too many people. When the end came, it was almost a case of feast to famine overnight. The bottom dropped out, and what small hopes were held for recovery were wiped out when the tourists came that season and refused to buy at any price a piece of real estate that they might have fought to own a few months before."

George Youngberg and Earl Aumann describe something similar in the Brotherhood of Locomotive Engineers' newly founded city of Venice: "The

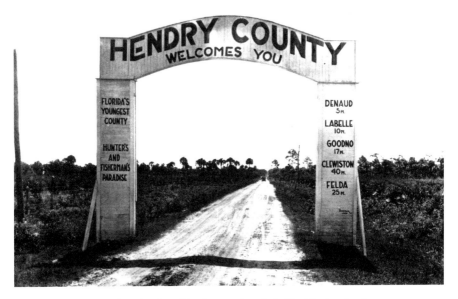

By 1928, large tracts of undeveloped lands were for sale in Florida, but few buyers were willing to take a chance on spending money on an uncertain future, and these tracts lay undisturbed until the post–World War II economic resurgence. *Courtesy of the Wynne Collection.*

new city of Venice developed like magic. Within three years the virgin land, where Venice now stands, was cleared, drained and graded. Streets were built and beautiful homes, apartments, hotels and business blocks were constructed. Industries were established. The community was incorporated as the City of Venice on May 4, 1927. The BLE Realty Corporation spent several million dollars besides the original purchase price of the land." Hundreds of people visited in the next two years, and the boom continued into 1928.

But the slowdown soon came, and the assessed value of property began dropping like the proverbial stone. Construction continued for a little while longer, but soon streets were stopped when only half completed and the workforces dwindled away. "Reluctantly," Youngberg and Aumann noted, "the BLE Realty Corporation gave up after four years of intense effort with the loss of $18 million." It was a common story throughout Florida and other boom time areas.

Historian Brian Rucker, in his *Floradale: The Rise and Fall of a Florida Boom Community*, describes what happened to that Panhandle community even though it had the backing of a famous family like the Ringlings. In 1925, Richard T. Ringling, a part owner of the family's circus business, and

William I. White purchased the lands once owned by the Porter interests, roughly fifty thousand acres in northern Santa Rosa and Okaloosa Counties. Ringling already had an interest in Montana, where he raised Holstein cattle, and White was the owner of the one-thousand-acre Willinga Poultry Farm in California. Both hoped to attract a number of farmers who were willing to farm the undeveloped land in northern Florida. White had already been active in the "home-on-the-land" movement in California and was on the board of the Landholders League of America, which hoped to attract Wall Street money to fund agricultural ventures like his.

The "Floradale Plan" developed by these men and their partners was focused on "diversified" agriculture that not only encouraged poultry and cattle raising but also promoted the Satsuma orange culture and the commercial growing of blueberries. Among the other buildings constructed by Ringling & White, as the firm was called, was a large hotel, the Granada, to promote interest in their proposed colony. They did have some success with the poultry part of the business, the Kea-Ring Poultry Farm, but the venture simply did not catch on with potential buyers. By 1928, the project was doomed as the land boom faded into memory. The more than one-half million dollars expended on the power plant, water tower and the Hotel Granada went for naught as these facilities simply sat idle. The Hotel Granada, like another Ringling venture in Sarasota, the Ritz Carlton, never opened its doors to the public. In the winter of 1930–31, the Missouri State Life Insurance Company foreclosed on the mortgage for the property and sold it for a mere $75,000. Later, the downhearted Richard Ringling visited his Montana property with his sister, and on August 31, he died of an apparent heart attack. He was only thirty-six years of age.

Elsewhere, the small town of Astor on the St. Johns River, long associated with the famed New York family of the same name, was rapidly feeling the effects of the land "bust." At the height of the boom, newly constructed roads brought many people to the area, and hopes were high for further development. In 1926, the famed Astor Bridge was built crossing the St. Johns River, and Highway 17 was built connecting Orlando to Jacksonville. A new highway connected Astor to Umatilla, skirting around the Ocala National Forest, then under development. Things appeared to be ready to boom.

When the boom collapsed, the traffic dwindled, the lands did not sell and the growth of new settlers and businesses stagnated. The development of the roads meant a slow end to the famed river traffic that had nourished the small town, and the trains passing through failed to slow down because there was no reason to do so. By 1928, according to A. Wass de Czege's *The History of Astor on the St. Johns*, Astor Park and surrounding areas were abandoned, "taking away the telephone and telegraph connections between Astor and the rest of the world." The demise of Astor may have been best symbolized by the burning of the famed Astor House hotel in the same year. The railroad depot was soon replaced by a boathouse, and automobile traffic slowed to a trickle. By 1931, many new residents were forced to leave their Astor homes in search of employment, and those who stayed hung on only by the proverbial skin of their teeth.

The stories of Astor, Floradale, Venice and Delray Beach reflect only parts of the struggle that awaited Floridians during the Great Depression. Proposed towns and cities in Florida failed to materialize as the dreamers had visualized, and many a wealthy man and woman who had succumbed to the lures of speculation felt the sting of the depression and collapse. Larger, more glamorous developments also fell to the pressures of poor credit, lack of cash and natural disasters. Joseph Young's great dream of Hollywood-by-the-Sea was essentially crushed by the impact of the hurricane of 1926. Although Miami and other parts of northern Dade County suffered severely, many forget that most of southern Broward County and, to some extent, Palm Beach County, also were devastated by the storm. These areas had only just

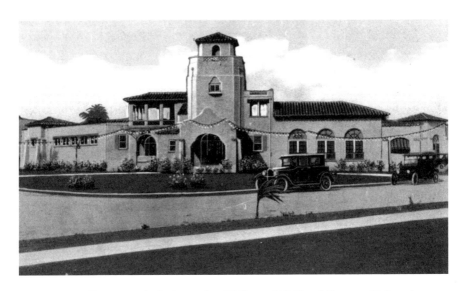

Joseph Wesley Young, who built the opulent Hollywood Golf and Country Club as the centerpiece of his new city of Hollywood, faced financial ruin after the hurricane of 1926. The hurricane of 1928 finished his career as a Florida developer. *Courtesy of the Richard Moorhead Collection.*

started to rebuild when the 1928 storm hit the mainland of Florida and caused even more wreckage and ruin. Long before the stock market crash of 1929, Florida had experienced what the rest of the nation was soon to feel.

People had a difficult time trying to make ends meet during the Depression, and it showed in hundreds of memoirs, letters and diaries from the period. Many of the letters to the governors of Florida and Eleanor Roosevelt were collected by Elna C. Green for her book, *Looking for the New Deal: Florida Women's Letters during the Great Depression*, and deal with the loss of money from the collapse of the local banks. Most of the bank failures in Florida were state-chartered banks. In Florida, banks that were part of the federal system, although weakened by the onslaught, rarely failed. Indeed, only eight such banks were permanently shut down, mostly because they were in rural areas with too much of the bank's capital tied up in property or assets such as tractors, automobiles and farming equipment. Shrinking household budgets and plunging crop prices prevented loan holders from paying off their loans, and the resale market for repossessed farm equipment was nonexistent.

The state banks "regulated" by Comptroller Ernest Amos had a much greater failure rate, mostly caused by speculation in land and loans to officers and directors of the banks themselves. The closing caught many depositors by surprise, and they wrote letters to the governors of Florida seeking some kind of resolution of their problem or assistance in meeting financial obligations. Annie E. Bartenfels of Miami wrote to Governor Carlton, "Pardon the liberty I take in writing you in regard to my personal affair concerning the Bank of Biscayne Bay (a state bank), which closed its doors June 11, 1930." Mrs. Bartenfels had deposited all of her savings in this bank, but all her frugality went for naught when the bank closed its doors. She was forced to work as a domestic worker (while that lasted) just to make ends meet. Similar stories came into the governor's office throughout the Depression, most with the same pathetic tale of bank closings and the loss of savings.

The frequency of requests for widow's pensions or relief for the elderly was also very high. Geraldine Peacock wrote to Carlton that the problem was not only a state problem but also one of great local concern. County, city and special districts had overcommitted their financial resources to development during the boom, and now that came back to haunt them and their citizens. Mrs. Peacock's case was not unusual: "I received your reply and did as you advised. And the county commissioners told me they could not help me in no way for the county is owing too much borrowed money. They told me I deserved a Pension." Yet, even though the commissioners felt her case was good, they could not provide the payments she expected. Mollie Jernigan of Munson, in the Panhandle, wrote to Carlton asking for a widow's pension and noted that she had seen many women in her neighborhood, most as well off or better than her, receiving the same. She too went to the board of county commissioners for a hearing, but they "did not donate [her] any thing." Pensions of any kind were difficult to collect on during these difficult times, and hundreds of letters like these found their way to the desks of political leaders.

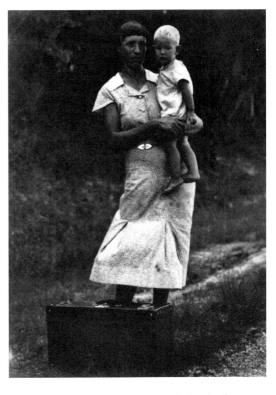

Women faced the greatest hardships during the Great Depression. Often they were faced with raising families alone when they were widowed or abandoned by their husbands. This woman and her child look for rides along the roadside as she moves to find family or work elsewhere. *Courtesy of the Ewart "Doc" Hendry Collection.*

Lila Robinson, who taught school on an island off the coast near Yankeetown (Point Ingles), wrote to Governor Sholtz that she was a widow with eight children and that her late husband had been shot and killed in the line of duty as a deputy sheriff. She worked in an area that survived through fishing, and many of her neighbors "just barely makes a living." One of her children, a boy of fifteen, had been tortured and burned by some men who doused him with gasoline. Although the men were caught and jailed, their capture and prosecution did nothing to pay the extensive doctor bills that had accrued as a result of the attack. She not only asked the governor to see what he could do to get the bills paid but unselfishly asked him to also see what he could do for the people on the island. She wrote that they "needs help but I don't know how to get it or where. I have tried a few places," but apparently she had no luck in finding assistance. Mary Porter of Miami Beach had but one child, but her case was different in that she

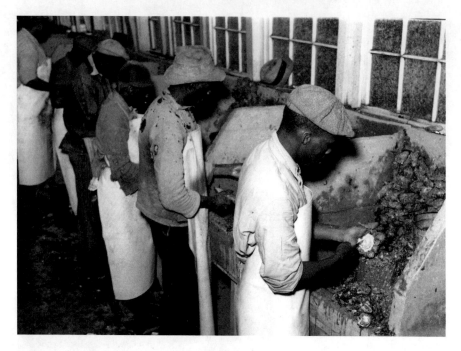

Workers along the coasts of Florida were often better off economically than workers in the interior of Florida. With little effort, they could survive off fish and oysters brought in each day, and some fishermen found a small, but constant, market for seafood. In this picture, workers shuck oysters for commercial sales. *Courtesy of the Wynne Collection.*

had "lost everything I ever saved in Miami." Her house had been taken over by the bank through foreclosure of "a big mortgage," and she had nowhere to turn. At sixty-eight years of age, she was near the end of her working life and was working as a live-in housekeeper in a Miami Beach hotel.

These letters were just a few of the many sent to Florida governors and to First Lady Eleanor Roosevelt. They make for emotionally draining reading, since most of the requests would never be met. It should also be noted that most of the letters were from women who were not afraid to work and had something to offer as workers. Few wanted anything like out-and-out charity, but there weren't any jobs to be had anywhere.

Rural life was stressful also, even though those who had land might be able to raise a crop or two, a vegetable garden and a few chickens or hogs. Gradually, however, even this source of sustenance began to dry up as sharecroppers and tenant farmers lost their lands under the federal programs to curtail crop production. Necessary seeds and fertilizers were often too expensive for marginal farmers to purchase. Many of the displaced farmers moved to towns and cities to try to find work, but they simply added to the numbers of unemployed there.

The outbreak of ticks and screwworms seriously impacted cattle ranchers in the Sunshine State. In his book, *Biscuits and 'Taters*, Manatee cattleman Joe Warner and his wife, Libby, discussed the impact of the cattle tick eradication program from their perspective in Manatee County. The program was necessary, Warner wrote, because the cattle simply died in the fields and watering holes because of the insects' bites. "Morgan Johnson," Joe writes, "remembered a time after one such winter (a cold, severe one), [when] he left his home on Braden River and rode to the Vanderipe ranch on the Miakka, and never was out of sight of a dead cow. Many of the live ones carried enough ticks on their bodies to fill a bucket." The state mandatory dipping program mandated that cows had to be dipped every two weeks, and range riders were hired by the state to assure that all the cattle were dipped. If any of the cattle were missed, these experienced cow hunters would track them down and either drive them to the vats or kill them on the spot. The state was supposed to pay three cents apiece for each cow dipped, but usually it was late in distributing the funds and issued scrip instead. This scrip was

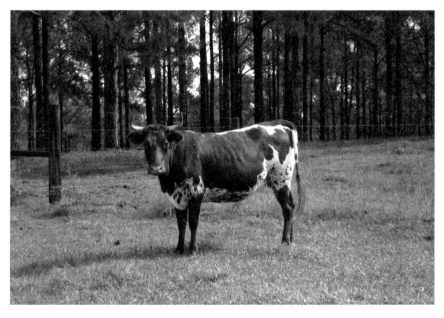

The Florida cattle industry, one of the mainstays of the state's economy, suffered greatly in the late 1920s and early 1930s as ticks, screwworms and other insect-borne diseases killed many cows. Fear of contagion from Florida cows closed the valuable Cuban market to imports from the Sunshine State. *Courtesy of the Wynne Collection.*

later traded in for bulls, saddles and other necessary ranching articles. One benefit brought by the eradication program, although many did not call it a benefit at the time, was the act of fencing in the cattle for better control. The days of the open-range cattle industry were numbered. The "biscuit and 'tater" time ended with the fencing laws too.

One of the persistent themes in most recollections of the period was the close cooperation individuals shared to simply survive. Ruby Chavous, quoted in an interview with Karen Voyles of the *Gainesville Sun*, put it very succinctly when she stated, "Having fun was always about being with other people, and that's what we did back then." Ralph "Rudy" Zadra noted in another interview that everyone played outside and used whatever came to hand: "If we had a tire to roll around, we would play service station." Marion County historian Sybil Bray recalled Ocala during the Depression: "On Wednesday afternoons, in the sleepy little town of Ocala, Florida, in the 1930's and 40's, the downtown merchants closed their doors. This was the mid-week break. The older folks rested, took naps and visited. The younger ones headed for Silver Springs for an afternoon of swimming and fun. Nothing can ever rival a swim in the cold clear waters of Silver Springs."

There were those who still believed in the Florida dream of the 1920s— one such dreamer was Albertino J. Beland, formerly of Quebec Province, Canada, who came to the United States in 1927. Fascinated by the freedom of movement and the large open spaces of the Sunshine State, he decided to build a new community that would appeal to the more contained and densely packed Canadians of his home province. In her book, *Belandville: A French-Canadian Colony in West Florida*, Laura Lee Scott described how Beland met and partnered with O.H.L. Wernicke, who knew of available land in northwestern Florida not far from the Alabama border in Santa Rosa County. After wiring each other about negotiations, Beland outlined his "Beland Plan" for developing the wilderness of northwestern Florida. He began by advertising the land in Canadian newspapers and, through a series of articles and pamphlets, began educating potential colonists on the whys and wherefores of growing food and obtaining other necessities in Florida. Working in conjunction with the Bagdad Land and Lumber Company, the holder of the titles to most of the lands, Beland welcomed the first 103 colonists to the property in June 1930. His plan called for thirty thousand acres to be bought and utilized by the colony. By the spring of 1931, the colony had planted vineyards, blueberries, blackberries and some pecan and Satsuma orange trees. Two years later, the community had grown to more than 550 colonists, and Beland boasted that the colony was prospering, debt free and providing an easy living for its residents. Three stores, a gas station, a post office, a hardware store, a church and a town hall were the main establishments in the colony, and plans were being made for a creamery, hosiery-knitting factory, poultry plant and hatchery. Additional plans were in the works for a meatpacking plant and a cannery for packing sweet pimento peppers.

By 1936, just five years later, the Beland colony had fallen on hard times. Difficulties in shipping agricultural products to market in a timely manner and the high costs of shipping destroyed all hopes for making a profit for the individual colonists. Prejudice against the French-speaking colonists led to conflicts with their American neighbors, and an internecine struggle over religion doomed the colony to failure. Many colonists, discouraged by the lack of markets, the failure to create an amicable social life and the general economic conditions caused by the Depression in the area, began leaving. Seventy-four of the properties were seized for taxes, and many of the younger men went into the nearby CCC camp in the Blackwater River National Forest. Some even ran into trouble with local law enforcement officials and were arrested for various charges, some obviously trumped up against the "foreigners." The dreams of A.J. Beland, like those of so many in those dark days, faded quickly during the reality of the Depression. He was surely not alone.

Life in Florida in the Depression presented many challenges, but it also produced many positive changes. The struggle to survive created common bonds among the poor, and the large number of people on relief or employed in make-work programs tended to erase some of the artificial divisions among classes. The Depression also refocused individual perceptions of what constituted essential needs for surviving and alerted that traditional employment patterns might have to be altered. Government programs, well meant and frequently well managed, did not answer all of the problems faced by the people of Florida. They would never be enough to bring back the prosperity of the early 1920s or to end poverty or put a chicken in every pot. Floridians, however, did not give up hope but tried to work out their own problems. They often triumphed when no one thought they could. It is this legacy of a generation that should be remembered most.

Chapter 6

NEW DEMANDS AND A GROWING LABOR SHORTAGE

Day by day now, the hordes of workers poured in. Some came limping in with their shoes and sore feet from walking. It's hard trying to follow your shoe instead of your shoe following you. They came in wagons from way up in Georgia and they came in truckloads from east, west, north and south. Permanent transients with no attachments and tired looking men with their families and dogs in flivvers.
—*Zora Neale Hurston,* Their Eyes Were Watching God *(1937)*

Beneath the surface of the idyllic picture of prosperity and growth painted by promoters and officials in the Sunshine State lurked another reality. By the mid-1920s, Florida agriculture was undergoing significant changes. Traditionally, the heart of farming in the Sunshine State had been limited to the counties in the Panhandle and a swath sweeping southward from Alachua and Marion to Hernando, Pasco and Lake Counties. By the beginning of the twentieth century, large portions of these lands were beginning to play out, losing their fertility because of constant use and poor farming practices. Tobacco, corn and cotton, which had constituted the bulk of crops produced in the state, were notorious for depleting soil nutrients and contributing to soil erosion. Farmers began to push cash crop cultivation farther southward and into marginal lands that once supported large forests. The thin topsoil of central Florida could no longer support such crops, and after only a couple of years, these lands were worthless.

Although cotton prices had increased dramatically from the low of 9.2 cents per pound in 1900 to more than 35 cents per pound in 1919, the end

New Demands and a Growing Labor Shortage

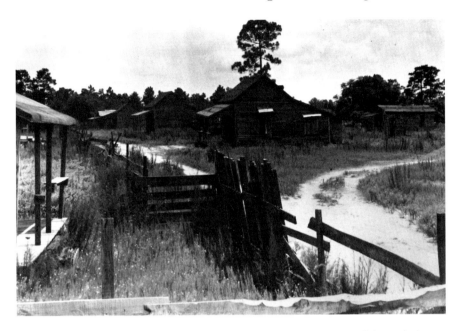

Falling crop prices and depleted soil led to the abandonment of many small farms during the 1930s. When these farms were abandoned, laborers and sharecroppers were thrown out of work and onto the unemployment rolls. *Courtesy of the Wynne Collection.*

of World War I saw a decrease in demand for the staple. Prices began a slow descent that continued until 1940, when World War II sent demand skyrocketing. As demand for cotton grew in the first two decades of the twentieth century, farmers hurried to bring new and marginal acreage into production. Annual yields per acre decreased because the "out" parcels could not support continued plantings, and erosion, which had been held in check by better practices on the older lands, became a real problem as the thin topsoil played out. It took more and more acres to maintain crop production each year, and when crop prices fell, the rate of farm foreclosures climbed during the 1920s, reaching a peak in 1927. Overall values for farmlands and farm buildings fell during the decade as well.

While specific figures for the Sunshine State are hard to find, the 1920s also saw a general decline in farm populations nationwide, falling from a high of 32.0 million persons in 1920 to a low of 12.6 million in 1930. Just as other states in the Union witnessed declining numbers of farmers and their families, so too did Florida. The number of farm laborers also fell during this period, moving from a high of 32.2 million in 1920 to only 12.5 million in 1930.

Although the rapid mechanization of farming in the Midwest and Southwest mitigated these figures somewhat, the southern region of the

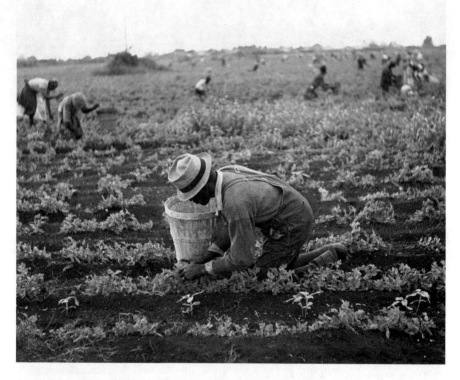

As small farms became inactive, corporations moved into agriculture in Florida and began cultivating large open fields in the southern parts of the state. Here, a migrant worker plants beans in a field near Arcadia. *Courtesy of the Library of Congress.*

United States, with its smaller fields and more diverse terrain, consistently represented the bottom tier of the economic picture. The initial costs of buying machines to compensate for declining labor pools, the costs of repair and maintenance and the costs of fuels to operate the machines proved too expensive for southern farmers, who continued to use mules and horses to pull plows and other implements. At least fodder to feed the animals could be grown at home, and the animals seldom needed repairing.

The small fields cultivated by farmers in Florida precluded the use of machinery, and for the first time in the history of the Sunshine State, cotton growers—and tobacco farmers as well—had to deal with a labor force that was growing smaller and smaller each year. Cotton farming was labor intensive and largely depended on the labor of landless African Americans.

New Demands and a Growing Labor Shortage

During the 1920s, thousands of black workers abandoned agriculture and headed north to industrialized states, seeking work in factories that paid better wages. The growth of the Ku Klux Klan, the growing rigidity of the Jim Crow system of segregation and the lack of political and economic opportunities were factors in persuading African Americans to head for cities in Ohio, Michigan, Illinois, Pennsylvania and New York. Between 1916 and 1921, more than 500,000 blacks, or about 5 percent of the African American population in the South, left the region for perceived greener pastures in the North. Like farmers in all the southern states, farmers in north Florida faced a growing labor shortage for the first time in the state's history.

One of the major reasons for this out-migration by Florida blacks was the failure of the "Florida movement," which historian Paul Ortiz deals with in depth in his 2006 book, *Emancipation Betrayed*. Returning veterans, infused with the ideals of democracy, challenged the white power structure in the Sunshine State—registering to vote, paying poll taxes and urging women to register for the first time—only to see their efforts frustrated by "official obstruction and massive violence." Faced with the determination of whites to deny them even modest political gains, many African Americans decided to "vote with their feet" and pulled up stakes and left with their families. Of

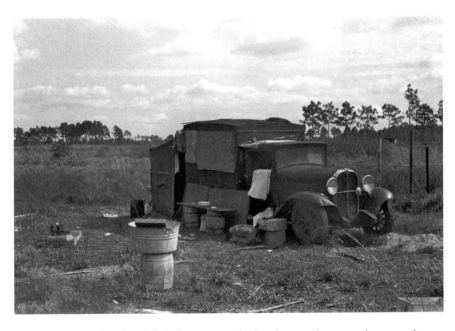

As small farmers abandoned their farms across the South, many became migrant workers. Many found jobs as itinerant citrus workers and day laborers in the muck fields of the Sunshine State. *Courtesy of the Library of Congress.*

all workers in agricultural occupations in the Sunshine State, the percentage of African Americans fell from a high of 51 percent in 1910 to 42 percent in 1930. This was a trend that continued throughout the Depression.

Because agriculture was the primary source of wealth for the state's economy, business and political leaders looked for new sources of arable land and new sources of black labor. They decided that the time had come to fulfill the ambitions of nineteenth-century entrepreneurs and drain the Everglades. Newly recovered lands, known as "muck" lands because of the thick, black soil that lay beneath, would provide tens of thousands of acres for the production of new food crops like green beans, celery, corn and sugar cane, which would provide jobs for thousands of farmworkers. Selling recovered lands would also provide significant new funds for the state's coffers, and Stockbridge and Perry estimated that in 1926 the state still owned enough potential muck farmland to enrich the state treasury by $130 million. Having made the commitment to draining the Everglades and eager to reap the rewards, the legislature went to work with a will.

Beginning in 1901, the legislature approved the Drainage by Counties Act, the first of laws aimed at opening the Everglades to farming. This law

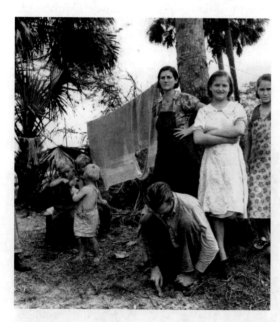

allowed landowners to petition county governments to build ditches, dams and canals and to issue bonds for that purpose. In 1903, the federal government conveyed a clear title to the Everglades to the state, and in 1905, a state Board of Drainage Commissioners was created to oversee drainage projects. In 1913, the legislature further broadened its efforts to spur agriculture in the muck lands of south Florida when it passed the General Drainage Act, which allowed landowners to petition for the creation of drainage districts. These acts came in recognition that the state's

Migrant workers with families in tow lived in primitive conditions in the agricultural fields of southern Florida, often living in lean-tos or makeshift sheds. *Courtesy of the Library of Congress.*

agricultural center had moved from the older plantation districts of north Florida to the southern part of the peninsula.

The drained lands provided muck and peat layers that ranged from two feet thick to as much as thirty feet in depth. Made up of decayed and decaying vegetation mixed with topsoil carried by feeder rivers and streams, the muck was so fertile that it produced four to five times the average yields for Florida lands. The moderate semitropical climate of southern Florida ensured that crops could be planted and harvested throughout the year, or at least that was the theory. While muck lands were much more fertile than the older cultivated lands in the northern and central parts of the state, farming them brought a whole new host of problems. Episodic rounds of drought and flooding combined with cold weather sometimes destroyed whole crops, while new insect threats created other hazards. Nevertheless, such was the belief in muck lands as the future of Florida agriculture, and resilient farmers persisted. Slowly, a pattern to successful farming emerged—large farms, mechanized farming and cash reserves were the only means of sustaining farming operations in the muck fields. Joseph Fink Jr., a resident of Indian River County, talked about the impact of opening the muck lands in a 1989 interview: "Father also farmed beans, peppers, [and] eggplants—garden vegetables. Back in the '30s when they opened up the Everglades, they put in big machinery to drain land. [They] put in thousands of acres of beans and other crops and pushed all the little farmers out of business. [We] couldn't compete with big farms."

Labor to replace the departed African American workers was not far away. Just eighty-five miles from West Palm Beach on the state's Atlantic coast were the Bahamas, an island chain with a large population of blacks willing to work in the vegetable and cane fields of the state. Bahamians had a long history of association with the Sunshine State, primarily in Key West and vicinity, and Henry Flagler had imported hundreds of Bahamian workers for his Florida East Coast Railroad. As the large muck farm economy began to develop in the early twentieth century, Bahamians were recruited to clear new fields and to plant and harvest crops. "Bahamians were welcomed," wrote Michael Craton and Gail Saunders-Smith in their 1998 history, *Islanders in the Stream: A History of the Bahamian People*, "for their skills, their willingness to work hard for comparatively low wages, their general cheerfulness, and because they caused less trouble than American blacks." So many islanders came to Florida that the commissioner of the island of San Salvador complained that there were no unmarried Bahamian men left on that particular island. By 1920, Bahamian immigrants accounted for more than 50 percent of Miami's black population. The same year saw

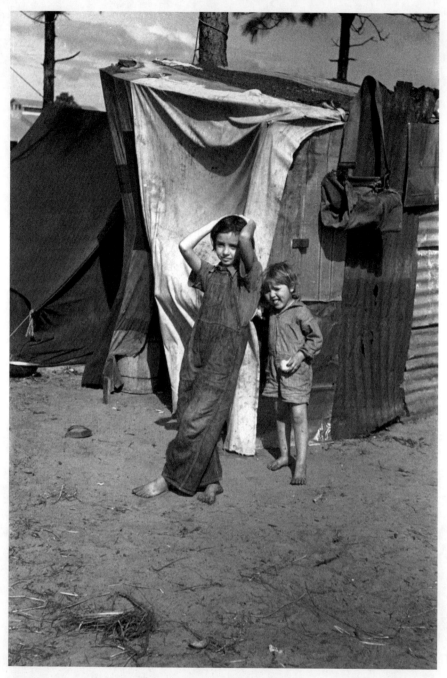

Children left alone while their parents work on the muck farms of south Florida. The open tin shed provides little protection against the heavy summer rains of the region. *Courtesy of the Library of Congress.*

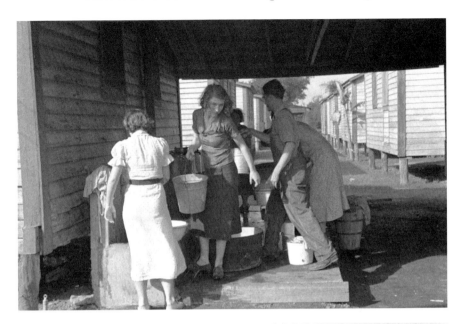

Above: Migrant families used whatever housing they could find. Many often shared housing with other migrant families, and housing could range from abandoned chicken coops to dilapidated house trailers or the insides of cars. *Courtesy of the Library of Congress*.

Right: While their husbands toiled in the muck fields, mothers were left with the task of supervising children who found little to do in the migrant camps. *Courtesy of the Library of Congress*.

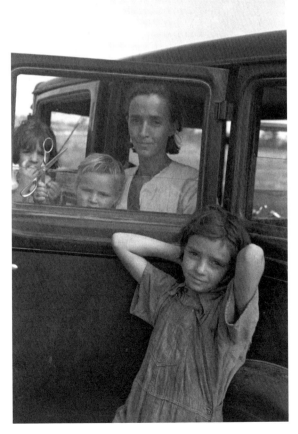

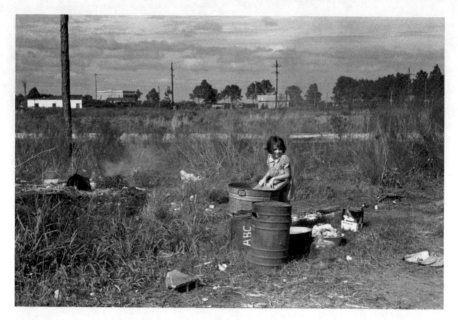

Life as a migrant worker was hard. Migrant families living in make-do shelters had little access to running water, electricity or other amenities. Mothers frequently worked in the fields beside their husbands, while children were left alone or in the care of older siblings. *Courtesy of the Library of Congress.*

immigrants from the islands send more than $100,000 in money orders back to their families, which helped fuel the moribund Bahamian economy.

Laborers—African Americans and poor whites—from northern Florida and other southern states also made seasonal journeys to the muck farms, preferring day labor and daily pay to sharecropping or tenant farming. As Hurston wrote in *Their Eyes Were Watching God*, they came "all night, all day, hurrying in to pick beans. Skillets, beds, patched up spare inner tubes all hanging and dangling from the ancient cars on the outside and hopeful humanity, herded and hovered on the inside, chugging on to the muck. People ugly from ignorance and broken from being poor."

The hurricanes of 1926 and 1928 struck the muck farming areas particularly hard. Of all the hundreds of casualties in the blow of 1928, the majority came from the low-lying muck farms that nestled against the dikes of Lake Okeechobee. The muck farms were not paradise, but they did offer farm laborers a chance to escape the grinding poverty and constant violence of the traditional farming areas of Florida. Of all the regions of the Sunshine State, the muck farms appeared to have had the best chances of escaping the full impact of the depression that was sweeping the state by the end of the decade.

Chapter 7
CATTLE AND CITRUS
PRICES TANK

My dad, he owned all the other range cattle here [Brevard County]. *They have some dairies, a bunch of dairies here, but nobody wanted to dip their cows, so they sold them cheap. They run from around $5 a head was all they was then. They were high back in '28 and '29, and the banks all went busted. Nobody had any money, so they'd take anything they could get.*
—Lester "Judge" Platt, quoted in Debra Wynne and Carolynn A. Washbon's
Judge Platt: Tales from a Florida Cattleman *(1998)*

In 1929, Florida was home to 355,000 beef cattle, valued at $23.40 per head. The annual yield of beef was estimated at 42 million pounds. By 1939, the number of beef cattle had increased to some 623,000, which produced 71 million pounds of meat for the market. Despite this tremendous increase in the number of cattle in the state and despite the increase in meat production, the value of individual heads of cattle had fallen to $20.50. During the 1930s, small cattle operations, like small farming operations, gave way to large corporate ranches, and, like farmers, cattle ranchers increased production to compensate for falling market prices.

Throughout the decade, state and federal regulations concerning tick and screwworm eradication were imposed on cattle production, "a very costly and expensive program especially since nobody had any money." The imposition of these regulations was not well received by cattlemen, as Gilbert Tucker wrote in his 2001 biography, *Before the Timber Was Cut*. "These old-timers," he wrote, "were certainly not use[d] to having bureaucrats tell[ing] them what they had to do to comply with state and federal regulations." Despite the opposition of cattlemen to dipping cows in vats of arsenic to get rid of the ticks and screwworms, they had little choice but to comply. Cuba, which was the major market for Florida cattle, imposed an embargo on shipments to the island nation, as did southern states like Alabama, Georgia and Mississippi. Until the tick and screwworm problems were solved, the largest markets for Florida cattle were closed.

Florida regulators and agricultural scientists attacked the tick and screwworm problems on several fronts before they found successful methods of dealing with it. "Judge" Lester Platt, a longtime cattleman, gave a vivid account of why Cuban and American beef buyers wanted nothing to do with Florida cattle and the difficulties involved in ridding cattle of the pests:

> *He'd* [a screwworm] *eat and stink; my god, them things stink. And what we did, we started out doctoring them* [cows], *pouring gasoline in the place* [where the screwworms were] *and picking them out with tweezers and burning them. That was a slow job, and then they finally come out. Well, we went to the place where you got your clothes done. You know, the dry cleaners. We got that benzoyl that they had, and we used that, and then we got just regular old tar, pine tar, and put it on the place, and that would keep them off. If there's a cut on him* [the cow], *you could put it there, and if he had screwworms, when you got through doctoring him—got them all out of there—why you poured tar in it or rubbed it in and rubbed it around and on the hair, and he wouldn't get back in there.*

While cattlemen worked on their home remedies, the University of Florida faculty experimented on more scientific approaches to ending the screwworm threat permanently. The most effective method proved to be the sterilization of female flies that laid the eggs that became the larval maggots. After a few abortive attempts—one release of millions of the female flies was a disaster because none of the flies were sterile—the program proved to be effective. By 1935, screwworms in Florida were largely a thing of the past.

Florida regulators also mandated a dipping program to combat the outbreak of ticks. The program was unpopular with cattlemen, but gradually and reluctantly they began to comply with the regulations. However, the cost in additional labor and supplies was prohibitive for some smaller ranchers, and they sold out to cattlemen with greater financial resources. In order to force compliance, the state hired its own cowhands to ride the open ranges of the state and round up cattle that had not been dipped. These

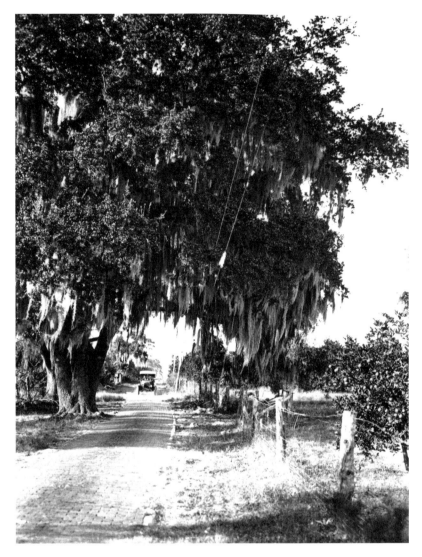

As a result of the state's mandate to dip all cattle in arsenic vats and the imposition of steep financial penalties for noncompliance, Florida ranchers began the expensive process of fencing their pastures, although a state law requiring fencing would not be enacted until the late 1940s. *Courtesy of the Wynne Collection.*

cattle would then be taken to a state-operated vat and dipped. For each cow dipped in these vats the owner was charged two dollars, an exorbitant sum since the price of an individual cow was only eight to twelve dollars. The determination of state and local agencies to enforce the regulations on dipping led to confrontations between cattlemen and government agents. By

1935, ticks and screwworms were eradicated from Florida cattle herds, and even the most reluctant cattleman had to admit it was the best thing to have had happen to the cattle industry.

Citrus growers faced their own difficulties. In late 1928 and early 1929, infestations of the Mediterranean fruit fly attacked citrus groves near Orlando. Within a few months, the infestations had spread through most of the commercial groves in the state. In a desperate effort to control the outbreak, twenty thousand men were hired as a temporary labor force to destroy infected trees. Although the state was in dire financial straights, it nevertheless spent more than $281,000 in this effort, a sum that was nowhere near the more than $6 million spent by the federal government.

Housing developments, sold to investors in the 1920s with the promise that citrus groves located on individual lots would pay the mortgage, went broke overnight. Temple Terrace (near Tampa) and Howey-in-the-Hills (north of Orlando) were particularly hard hit. D. Collins Gillett, who shared the honor of being Tampa's greatest developer in the mid-1920s with D.P. Davis, lost everything as he saw the value of his Temple Terrace development plunge to almost nothing overnight. William J. Howey, the man behind Howey-in-the-Hills, managed to hang on to some land until his death in 1938. He died just before the U.S. Supreme Court ruled that citrus contracts were unregistered securities and therefore illegal. Gillett had been dead for several years by this time.

The quick actions to deal with the fruit fly infestations by the state and national governments were due, in large part, to the efforts of Jesse J. Parrish, a Brevard County legislator and president of the Senate. Parrish, who founded the Nevins Fruit Company (one of the first co-operatives in the state), had a reputation of "never losing a citrus battle in the Legislature." Although citrus production declined from twenty-eight million boxes shipped in 1929 to a mere eighteen million in 1930, a record thirty-five million boxes were shipped in 1931. By the next year, however, production had fallen once again. The state legislature passed the Citrus Commission Act in 1935, which mandated standards for commercial citrus and, more importantly, levied a tax on all boxes of shipped citrus. The tax was used to fund an advertising campaign to market the state's citrus crops.

Although the majority of small producers continued to rely on independent truckers to get their produce to market, state-funded agricultural inspection stations were established along major highways to ensure that all citrus leaving the state complied with the commission's regulations and kept the quality of produce leaving the state high. Although the Citrus Commission

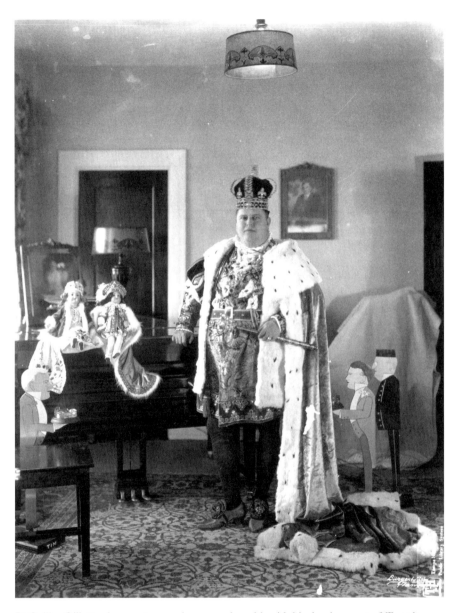

D. Collins Gillett, who rose to prominence and wealth with his development of Temple Terrace near Tampa, died in obscurity and poverty when the Florida boom became the Florida bust. *Courtesy of the Burgert Brothers Collection, Tampa Public Library.*

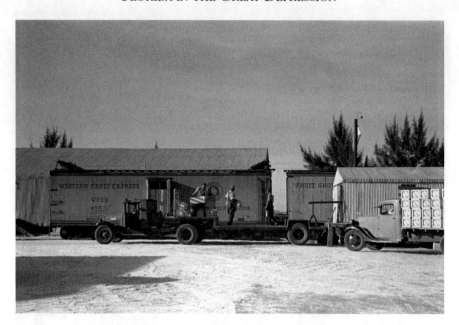

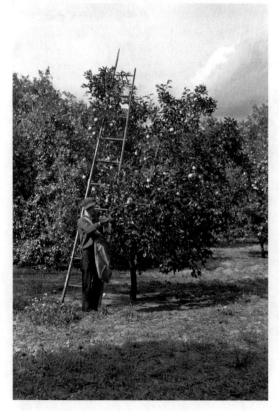

Above: Florida citrus, which recovered from the devastating Mediterranean fly outbreak in the late 1920s, was a stabilizing factor in the economy of the state during the height of the Depression. *Courtesy of the Library of Congress.*

Left: This migrant worker is busy harvesting oranges in Polk County in 1937. *Courtesy of the Library of Congress.*

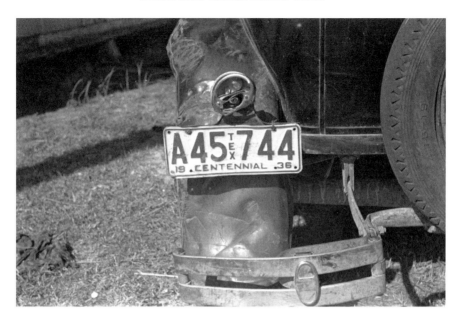

Migrant farm workers traveled throughout the Sunshine State in search of work. Some Florida workers made annual pilgrimages to states as far away as New Jersey and Michigan to harvest seasonal crops, while workers from other states migrated to Florida. *Courtesy of the Library of Congress.*

Act did not solve all of the problems of citrus growers—notably the annual surpluses and market fluctuations—the imposition of standards did bring stability and order to citrus production. By the mid-1930s, Florida had displaced California as the leading citrus-producing state, and in 1936, the total number of boxes reached forty million.

Like cattle ranchers and muck farmers, the major reason for the citrus industry's quick recovery, although with slow growth, was largely due to the willingness of small producers to accept industry standards and join with larger producers to form co-operatives. Of course, it did not hurt the industry to have powerful politicians strategically placed throughout the legislative branch of state—advantages small cotton and tobacco farmers did not enjoy.

Chapter 8
TIMBER, TURPENTINE AND FORCED LABOR

With the commissary we makes [sic] *a gross profit of sixty per cent and a net profit of twenty per cent. You know that's pretty good—it takes a slice offen the salaries. We don't hardly have to pay no salaries. The private stores around here do good to make five to eight per cent profit. Of course we have to charge the niggers* [sic] *more, but they save in the long run. Just think what it would cost them to drive thirty miles into town for vitals if they had cars.*
—*Stetson Kennedy,* Palmetto Country *(1942)*

Farming in the Sunshine State was not the only sector of the state's economy to suffer during the 1920s. Timbering and turpentining, which had long been mainstays in the rural counties of north and central Florida, were declining because of two factors—a decline in the numbers of laborers willing to work in the industries and the fact that too many trees were being cut or damaged by turpentining.

Between 1900 and 1925, Florida averaged more than one billion board feet of lumber each year, which meant that the state's forests were being decimated by overcutting. The land and building boom of the early 1920s had created a strong demand for lumber and lumber byproducts, so much so that sawmills ran from dawn to dusk to meet the calls for more and more lumber. Overnight, small settlements such as Centralia in Hernando County sprang up around isolated sawmills, quickly acquiring all of the refinements of a modern town—stores, schools, movie theaters, hotels, a post office and homes—all owned by the timber company. Centralia was "born" in 1910 and "died" in 1917. For

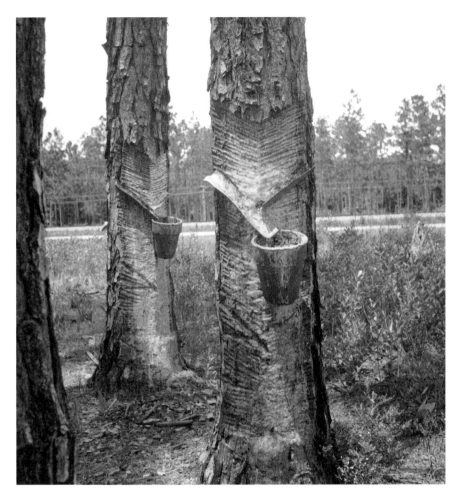

Thousands of "cat faces," areas where the tree bark had been removed to facilitate the flow of resin, marked the forest of northern Florida in the 1930s, but the industry was slowly vanishing as workers abandoned turpentining and as world markets changed. *Courtesy of the Library of Congress.*

seven years, the sawmill, owned by Edgar Roberts and his brother, produced up to 100,000 board feet of lumber each day, mostly cypress. Nearby, Lewis S. Petteway, a friend of the Roberts brothers, operated a turpentine still that employed several dozen men. At the height of its prosperity, Centralia could claim more than 1,500 residents, far more than the 500 inhabitants of Brooksville, the county seat. For the Robertses, the supply of timber seemed endless, and in 1917 the company had 160 acres covered with lumber fifteen feet high. Stan Weston, a Florida forester, described the process of clear-

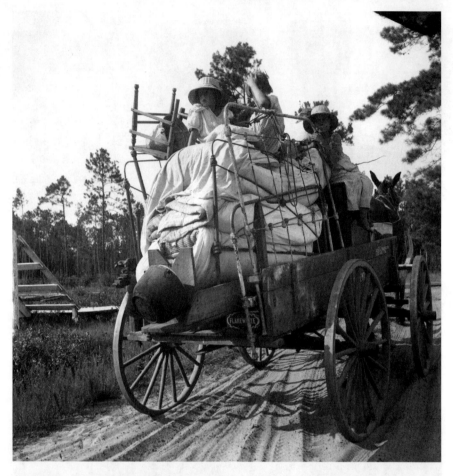

As logging and turpentine industries closed, the small company towns—often located deep in the forests—slowly died and became ghost towns. This 1936 photograph shows one family abandoning a turpentine town in north Florida. *Courtesy of the Library of Congress.*

cutting employed by the company: "No thought was given to the future of replenishing the forest. Was not this blanket of forest inexhaustible? Wasn't it a wasteland of wilderness, jungle, something to be removed so that 'civilization' might advance? Leave seed trees, plant new trees, and seedlings—ridiculous they thought. Never would this sea of virgin timber be exhausted. How wrong they were!" Weston was right. In 1917, when the Centralia mill owners could look out over acres of boards, they also had to face the reality that there were no more trees to cut.

Centralia was only one of a number of similar boomtowns created in the wilderness of Florida forest and abandoned when the timber was exhausted.

Timber, Turpentine and Forced Labor

It was a fate similar to that of Cedar Key, a small town on the Gulf coast that had thrived for several decades as the Eberhard Faber and Eagle Pencil Companies ruthlessly harvested the red cedar trees that grew in abundance in the area in the latter part of the nineteenth century. With little thought to reforestation, the company was forced to abandon its activities when the supply of trees ran out. By 1930, state officials listed more than sixteen million acres of former forestland denuded and worthless. Most of these former forests were simply left to bake in the hot Florida sun, slowly eroding as wind and rain took their tolls.

As stands of available timber became fewer and fewer, and as the Florida boom slowed and eventually died, many of the whites employed in timbering, as well as some African Americans, headed for the towns and cities of the state. Beginning in the 1920s, Florida saw a gradual population shift from rural to urban—a movement that would make the state 70 percent urban by the mid-1940s. As people moved to urban centers, available labor became scarcer in the countryside.

The decision by Governor Cary A. Hardee to end convict leasing by the state in 1919 created difficulties for the operators of mining and turpentine companies, although some leased convict labor could be had from counties that were still allowed to farm out their prisoners to private companies. Scandals over mistreatment of convicts, including several deaths, led the legislature to outlaw all convict leasing in 1923. Convicts in state prisons and county jails were put to work building or improving roads for the increasing number of automobiles that flooded roads in the Sunshine State—a practice that continues in a much-modified form today.

To assist the timber, naval stores, phosphate mining companies and even farmers that contracted for most of the state's 1,500 convicts, the same legislature strengthened the provisions of the Contract Law, which made leaving employment while still in debt to an employer prima facie evidence of intent to defraud. The result was an upswing in the number of instances of peonage, which was little more than debt slavery enforced by the threat of prosecution by local law enforcement agencies and the various courts. Most of the workers in turpentine camps were black; seldom did whites participate except in management positions. "The work is too severe and the pay too small for white workers," wrote Stetson Kennedy in *Palmetto Country*. "Too, there is a feeling among white workers that such disagreeable work was negroes' [*sic*] work, and that white men would demean themselves by doing it." Marcus Fagg, the Florida director of federal relief, noted that African Americans were "subject to economic oppression not infrequently

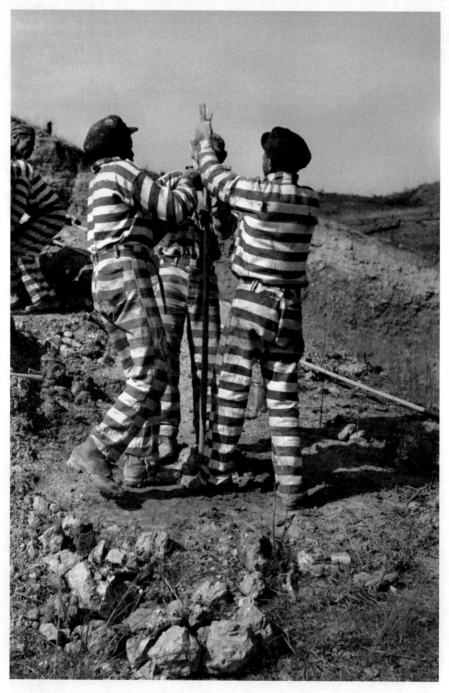

The loss of cheap convict labor for Florida logging and turpentine operators, following a number of scandals, severely restricted the forest industries in the Sunshine State and contributed to their eventual demise. *Courtesy of the Library of Congress.*

tantamount to peonage, particularly in the naval stores and lumbering industries." As such, he concluded, "Negroes live on a very low subsistence wage, even during prosperous times, and quickly fall in to a condition of actual want under adverse economic conditions."

Despite the widespread use of the Contract Labor Law and extralegal threats of violence, the reckless clear-cutting of the longleaf and slash pine forests, when coupled with the failure of timber companies to undertake massive reforestation efforts, meant that the turpentine business was slowly dying. The number of available working trees diminished rapidly. This also coincided with a decline in the demand for naval stores products. Unlike the citrus industry, timber companies and turpentine operators did not see the need for taking collective action, regulating cutting or mandating reforestation.

The growing failures of Florida timber and naval stores operations added to the economic woes of the state.

Chapter 9
RACE AND THE URBAN MIGRATION

The men wanted to work. This was the dominant theme through all the years of the Depression. I very seldom found a man who was willing to accept relief as a process of life. He knew it was debilitating. I'll never forget the morning we opened the [relief] office. It was a cold November day, 1930. Thousands of men were lined up for blocks. Many were skilled men and carried their tools with them. In the course of that winter, we put almost ten thousand men to work.
—*Dr. Martin Bickham, quoted in Studs Terkel's* Hard Times: An Oral History of the Great Depression *(1970)*

During the boom of the 1920s, civic leaders in the Sunshine State boasted about the tremendous growth that the state and cities were experiencing in population. Overall, the state added a remarkable 29 percent increase in permanent residents—four times the national average. Individual cities, some of which were new in origin, sustained even higher rates, such as Miami's increase of 165 percent between 1920 and 1925. Only Jacksonville, which experienced little in the way of speculative development, lagged behind, recording only a 3 percent growth during the period. The rapid growth that made city fathers so proud during the first half of the decade would present many difficulties to them for the next fifteen years.

CITY GROWTH IN FLORIDA, 1920–1925

CITY	1920	1925	INCREASE
Tampa	51,608	94,808	84%
Jacksonville	91,558	94,206	3%
Miami	29,571	71,419	141%
Lakeland	7,062	17,064	142%
Orlando	9,282	22,272	140%
West Palm Beach	8,659	19,132	121%

Faced with no jobs and few ways to sustain themselves on farms, agricultural workers in Florida (frequently joined by small farmers) made their way to the cities and towns, looking for work—anything at all to feed their families—but there was little employment to be found. Many of these displaced workers were African Americans whose presence in Florida cities severely strained race relations for the next decade. No relief program for the unemployed was free from racism, nor were government reductions in spending. Whenever relief programs were funded, blacks received smaller payments. Whenever jobs were available, African Americans were the last hired and the first fired. Although blacks made up only 29 percent of the state's population, they received nearly 46 percent of the relief monies expended in the Sunshine State.

The influx of rural people into the cities and towns of the Sunshine State further depressed the labor market as lessening market demands for manufactured products and the movement toward mechanization resulted in layoffs and factory closings. Tampa, which had been the center of cigar production during the last two decades of the nineteenth century and the first two decades of the twentieth century, had witnessed labor upheavals and strikes since before World War I. Cigar factory owners, who saw the markets for their products decline rapidly, searched for ways to produce cigars more cheaply and turned to mechanization. Latin workers, who had long prided themselves on their skills at rolling fine cigars, took to the streets in protest and closed the factories. When the factories reopened, machines had replaced many of the workers, putting thousands out of work. Although a few of these newly unemployed set up "buckeyes," or independent shops, the majority were forced to seek employment in other fields.

When Marcus C. Fagg issued a report on relief operations in Florida in October 1935, he paid special attention to unemployed Latinos, particularly those in Tampa. "Temperamentally and racially these people

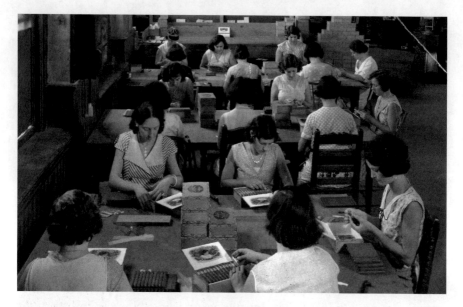

Florida's cigar industry, beset by labor strikes in the 1920s and 1930s, experienced a downturn during the Depression. To reduce costs and labor strife, cigar factory owners turned to mechanization, although some jobs still required humans. In this 1937 photograph, women inspect and package cigars in a Tampa factory. *Courtesy of the Library of Congress.*

represent a difficult problem, and in Tampa, where they form a considerable bloc in local politics, communistic and other radical activities have necessitated tact and clear thinking on the part of relief administrators."

Poor whites, who constituted "a considerable portion of the population in North and Northwest Florida," also received special notice in Fagg's report. "These people," he wrote, "many of them illiterate, who existed until the advent of modern roads under almost primitive social and economic conditions, live in the more remote backwoods districts. They are notoriously shiftless and lazy, although these characteristics may be due to the offsets of hookworm, pellagra, and malaria. It is not strange that this class of people, long accustomed to a minimum standard of living, should flock to relief offices when word drifted into the woods that the government was giving away food and 'cash money.'"

Florida's largest city, Jacksonville, had escaped many of the problems brought about by rapid growth in the first half of the 1920s—but it too would witness a similar influx of unemployed persons from the countryside. The city had long been the major market for naval stores and timber, but the collapse of these industries meant that thousands were out of work, and they headed to the nearest metropolis. To these thousands were added other

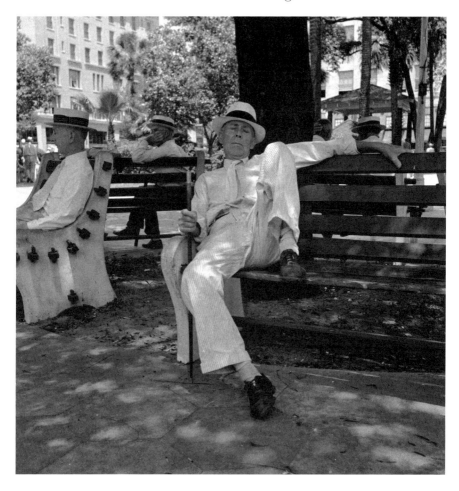

Jacksonville, Florida's largest city, provided work for many unemployed individuals with money contributed by industrialist Alfred I. du Pont. Most of the work consisted of keeping the streets and parks clean. In this 1937 photograph, men can be seen taking advantage of the peaceful park setting. *Courtesy of the Library of Congress.*

thousands of small cotton and tobacco farmers, forced to abandon their farms by adverse market conditions and foreclosures. Unable to borrow funds to continue farming operations, they packed up their belongings and headed for Jacksonville. There they joined hundreds of unemployed shipyard workers, cigar makers and port workers.

Jacksonville was unusual. Well-known civic leader and businessman Alfred I. du Pont, well aware of the problems faced by the unemployed, established a private public works program similar to one he had created in Wilmington, Delaware. Out-of-work men were hired to sweep streets, maintain public parks and perform other chores for minimum wages. Although there were a limited number of jobs available through this charitable undertaking, for the lucky few who were able to participate, the money they made often was the difference between feeding their families and not eating.

FLORIDA PER CAPITA INCOME, 1929–1935

YEAR	PER CAPITA INCOME
1929	$510
1930	$478
1931	$392
1932	$317
1933	$289
1934	$328
1935	$352

One response to the growing number of unemployed in Florida cities was the creation of radical groups of whites determined to preserve the few available jobs for white men. James D. Patterson, in *The Education of Blacks in the South, 1860–1935,* noted the change in southern perceptions of what were proper jobs restricted to African Americans and those reserved for whites. Driving a garbage truck or digging ditches was no longer considered demeaning for whites. In Jacksonville in 1926, the Blue Shirts, a Ku Klux Klan clone whose virulent rhetoric was aimed at African Americans, demanded that all new jobs be reserved for whites and that blacks currently working should be immediately replaced by white men. *The Blue Shirts,* an anti-Negro newspaper published by the organization, sought to rouse white anger and to intimidate employers. Those employers who failed to comply with the group's demands were identified by name as "nigger lovers" in the publication. In Tampa, a fascist group, the Silver Shirts, which had chapters in other American cities such as Detroit, espoused similar ideas and embarked on the same kind of campaign. Florida cities were not alone in having to deal with such groups. In 1927, Atlanta saw the rise of the Black Shirts, who staged marches demanding the dismissal of black workers and their replacement by whites.

According to Charles S. Johnson, a field investigator for the Rosenwald Fund, which funded secondary education of blacks in the South, the changes brought about by the Depression "placed white and Negro workers more acutely in competition for the same jobs, particularly on city, county, and state work where political influence can grant favors to voters and receive votes in return." Jessie O. Thomas, a prominent educator at Atlanta University, noted "a complete reversal of the white South toward menial labor. A white man at the present time has no fear of losing his social cast[e] because he digs a ditch, [or] drives a garbage or scavenger truck." Similar observations were made by African American educators throughout the southern states. This "enforced unemployment" of African Americans led to other problems for southern cities, such as an increase in crime

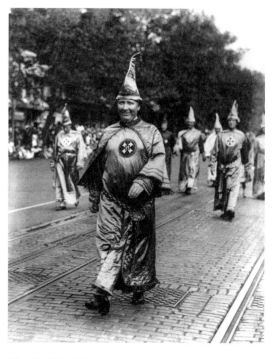

The Ku Klux Klan remained active in Florida during the 1930s, even after it had lost membership nationally following a number of scandals. Klan members marched often in the streets of the Sunshine State cities and kept a close eye on hiring practices by private businesses. *Courtesy of the Library of Congress.*

and juvenile delinquency among the black population.

The depressed economy proved to be fertile soil for the growth of extremism. The sensational publicity generated by the trial of nine African American teenage boys for rape in Scottsboro, Alabama, was used by the American Communist Party (which provided the legal defense for the accused) to recruit black members. Elsewhere, the Ku Klux Klan, which claimed a national membership of four to five million in 1926, maintained a forceful public presence, although leadership scandals would diminish its national presence by 1930. Nevertheless, the Klan remained active, and membership did not decline in the Sunshine State during the decade.

By February 1931, the unemployment situation was desperate in the urban areas. Seventeen of Florida's sixty-seven counties had inaugurated some kind of public welfare programs, although they were initially created to serve the unemployable. Gradually the focus of these agencies centered on helping the unemployed. Other cities joined Jacksonville in creating public works or relief programs—Tampa, Pensacola, West Palm Beach, Daytona Beach, Fort Myers, Lake Worth, Lakeland, Orlando and St. Petersburg offered small, underfunded programs. The massive bonded debts of cities, created in the early 1920s to fund improvements, and restrictions in city charters worked to limit available funding.

Where funding did exist, the recipients of relief received, on average, about $2.39 a month for an entire family, although this amount increased slowly. By March 1934, families received an average of $18.46 per month in federal relief dollars.

LENGTH OF RESIDENCY FOR FLORIDA RECIPIENTS OF PUBLIC ASSISTANCE, 1928–1933

LENGTH OF RESIDENCY	PERCENTAGE OF RECIPIENTS
25 years or more	29%
10 to 25 years	35%
boom years (1923–1928)	20%

LENGTH OF RESIDENCY (65 AND OLDER)	PERCENTAGE OF RECIPIENTS
50 years or more	38%
11 to 49 years	39%
10 years or less	23%

By 1933, 22 percent (226,868) of Florida whites were receiving some form of public assistance, while 36 percent (155,239) of African Americans were on relief. These numbers continued to rise over the next three years. The statistics for African Americans were skewed somewhat by the Great Migration of the 1920s, by the practice of having local relief committees determine who was eligible for relief and by the fact that blacks were a minority in the state. Unemployment was no respecter of place or persons. In nine of the state's sixty-seven counties, more than 40 percent of the population was on public assistance, while in a dozen other counties one-third were on the relief rolls. The numbers of recipients were split evenly between population centers—one-third came from rural areas and towns with populations under 500, while another one-third came from cities of 100,000 or more. The remaining one-third was in towns and counties with medium-sized populations. Length of residency in Florida was not a major factor in who received public assistance, although newer residents

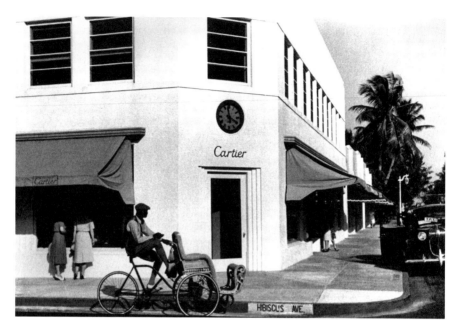

Wealthier Floridians, such as habitués of Palm Beach, Miami and Vero Beach, experienced little of the Great Depression, and for them, life went on as usual. *Courtesy of the Wynne Collection.*

(who constituted the smallest group in the state) did make up the smallest percentage of recipients.

State political leaders were slow to recognize the severity of the unemployment crisis faced by the state's citizens. In the late 1920s, leaders tended to dismiss the collapse of the state's economy as a temporary aberration that would quickly be corrected. The idea of using public funds to provide relief to the unemployed was an anathema to them and a clear rejection of the American concept of the "rugged individual." If people were out of work, they reasoned, it was because of personal failings and not the fault of the capitalist system.

Florida certainly represented the two extremes of the Depression years. In Miami, Palm Beach and even newly incorporated Vero Beach, those individuals who had money and had not gotten caught up in land speculation or buying stocks on the margin noticed little difference in their lifestyles. Many members of the "solidly" middle class experienced only slight changes in their standard of living. Charlie McClure, a Vero Beach pharmacist, noted, "It did not affect me. There was not enough people [in Vero Beach] to be affected much. Well, the banks closed, but did it [the Depression] come uptown, I would say no." Anne Keen, another Vero Beach resident, had a different take on the Depression's impact: "[There were] no apples [for sale on the streets] or food lines, but Mother and Dad (who operated a dairy) gave away a lot of milk, [they] couldn't collect bills anyway." Anne was a member of the District Welfare Board, and she related how one of her fellow members of the board, Skippy Hubbard, appreciated the free milk the Keen dairy gave away. "Outside of the fish Dad caught," she quotes Hubbard as saying, "and the milk your father gave us, I don't know what we would have done."

The massive downward spiral of the stock market, which began on October 24, 1929, and continued for the next week, brought reality home to Florida politicians. Herbert Hoover, who had parlayed the Republican claims of "Coolidge Prosperity" into an electoral success in the Sunshine State, had been president less than a year. When the full impact of the Depression hit throughout the United States in 1930–31, Hoover, who had headed relief efforts in Belgium and Germany after World War I, appeared to be tone-deaf when it came to the cries for assistance by his fellow Americans. An engineer by training, he appeared to have learned little about the operations of American business during his eight years as secretary of commerce. Caught between the demands of states and individuals for rapid and decisive actions to reverse the economic downfall, Hoover tended to side with men of wealth who railed against any kind of government interference in the economy.

Florida's conservative governor, John W. Martin, who was succeeded in 1929 by Doyle Elam Carlton, agreed with the business community and did little to relieve the suffering of citizens of the Sunshine State. Carlton was a conservative but one who favored tighter banking regulations, smaller government and the elimination of some government functions. He also favored a two-cent tax on gasoline, which he wanted to use to reduce the indebtedness of county governments. This measure was approved in a special session of the legislature in June 1929. In 1931, Florida legislators managed to enact, over the governor's initial veto, a law legalizing pari-mutuel gambling, which generated an additional $737,301 in income. Of this, half went into the state's coffers, while the other half was distributed equally among the state's sixty-seven counties. All in all, the Carlton administration had made little difference in righting the economy of the Sunshine State.

Within his own cabinet, Hoover was surrounded by men of wealth who urged him to leave the economic recovery to the same men who had created the mistakes that led to the Depression. Secretary of the Treasury Andrew W. Mellon, who had served in that position since 1921, informed reporters that, despite the collapse of the stock market and the rising rates of unemployment,

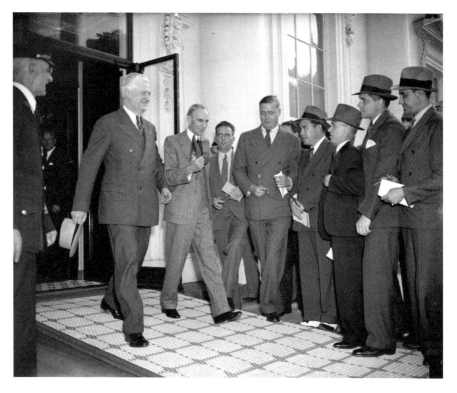

Automobile magnate Henry Ford won few friends or supporters when he offered to the unemployed his gratuitous advice on how to survive during the Depression. *Courtesy of the Library of Congress.*

he saw "nothing in the present situation that is either menacing or [which] warrants pessimism." Bowing to pressure from the business community, he signed the Smoot-Hawley Tariff Act in June 1930, which established exorbitant protective tariffs on foodstuffs and manufactured goods coming into the United States. The enactment of the Smoot-Hawley Tariff provoked a round of similar tariffs by other countries, and international trade—which the United States had dominated for years—ground to a halt, thus exacerbating the depression of the nation's economy.

As late as February 1931, Hoover issued a statement that he was opposed to using federal funds to provide relief to the unemployed and destitute. Instead, he argued that the proper ways to deal with the problems were individual actions, the assumption of assistance by local governments and through the "mutual self-help" of charitable organizations. Hoover was merely parroting the beliefs of leading businessmen who viewed the creation of a relief system— the dole—as the first step in creating a permanent class of unemployed persons, who would lose all incentives for working. Henry Ford was just one of the leading industrialists who opposed unemployment compensation, and in 1932, he offered his own solution. "No unemployment insurance can be compared to an alliance between a man and a plot of land," he wrote for the *Literary Digest*. "With one foot in industry and another foot in the land, human society is firmly balanced against most economic uncertainties. With a job to supply him with cash, and a plot of land to guarantee him support, the individual is doubly secure. Stocks may fail, but seedtime and harvest do not fail." He went on to say, in 1934, that "the depression was just a state of mind. It is over for everyone who has changed his state of mind." Ford failed to take into consideration two basic facts—eight million men and women had no jobs and, as a result, had no money to invest in farming, even on a small scale. As far as changing their "state of mind," citizens found this hard to do while facing homelessness and starvation.

Hoover, like Ford, could only offer advice. In 1931, he appointed Colonel Arthur Woods, a World War I hero, to head up the Emergency Committee for Unemployment. The committee, which had no funds to distribute, was little more than a cheering squad that offered advice to local governments. T.T. Craven, the head of the Federal Coordinating Service, sent a directive to the committee instructing it to avoid any reference to the federal government "both directly and by implication" because "the problem of relief is local and personal and this service is being used as a channel of communication only."

Thus, Hoover's program of doing nothing and leaving recovery to the business community resulted in a dramatic rise in the unemployed—from four million in 1929 to over eight million in 1931. Florida was not alone in facing massive unemployment; every state was affected. While the Hoover administration did little to nothing to resolve the crisis, average American families faced deepening poverty and suffering.

Throughout the United States, the unemployed gathered in newly created slums—called "Hoovervilles"—and waited for something to change. These poverty-stricken wretches were ripe for radical political change, argued some of the more thoughtful men of the times. "Gentlemen," Columbia University president Nicholas Butler warned his friends in the business community, "if we wait too long [to do something], somebody will come forward with a solution we may not like."

Chapter 10
HOOVER AND THE "NO DEAL"

I become frantic when I see my children without shoes, clothes, and proper nutrition—when I think of the great amount of food rotting away in warehouse while my children go to bed without eating. My blood boils within me against those who are responsible for such injustice in the world. Everything should be distributed equitably, and not go only to a few millionaires who exploit the productive class to enrich themselves.
—*Ybor City mother, quoted in Stetson Kennedy's* Palmetto Country

Herbert Hoover was perhaps the most reviled politician in America in 1932. His name had become synonymous with the poverty of the Depression, and jokes of all kinds made the rounds among the ranks of the unemployed. Buzzards were often referred to as "Hoover chickens," while jackrabbits were popularly called "Hoover hogs." In Florida, manatees became "Hoover cows" and were placed on the menus of poor families. Throughout the nation, references to "Hoover blankets"—newspapers used by the homeless to provide a little warmth on cold nights—were joined by jokes about "Hoover flags": pockets turned inside out to show how empty they were. On the vaudeville stage, in newspapers and in private conversations, Hoover's reputation, once so proudly discussed for his relief work in Europe, was now tarnished by his inability to abandon the tenets of free market capitalism or to intervene on behalf of the suffering millions of Americans. Arthur M. Schlesinger, commenting on Hoover's memoirs, noted that twenty years after the end of his presidency, the former president

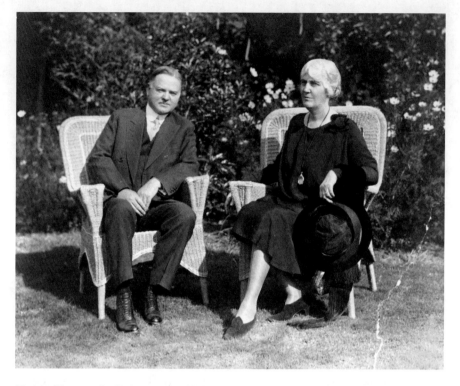

Herbert Hoover, who had won a landslide in the presidential election of 1928, quickly became a much-hated political leader as the Great Depression deepened in 1930 and 1931. In this photograph, he enjoys a moment in the White House garden with his wife. *Courtesy of the Library of Congress.*

"could see no mistakes committed during his presidency, no opportunities missed, no wrong guesses, nothing to regret."

Despite this later claim, he did begin to move slowly to alleviate the economic stagnation, but his programs were aimed at providing assistance to banks, insurance companies, agricultural mortgage associations and railroads. The first of these programs was the creation of the Reconstruction Finance Corporation (RFC), initially funded at $500 million but authorized to borrow up to $2 billion. Headed by Charles G. Dawes, the former vice president under Calvin Coolidge, the RFC took its mandate seriously and within six months had loaned more than $1.2 billion to various businesses, including a multimillion-dollar loan to Dawes's own bank. On February 27, three weeks after Congress authorized the RFC, it went further to approve the Glass-Steagall Act, which made an additional $750 million in gold bullion in loans to businesses to expand the currency. To most average Americans, Herbert Hoover was willing to go to any lengths to meet the demands of business but he was unwilling to do anything to help the average citizen. While no measure seemed too extreme in Hoover's support of business, his attitude toward providing some relief to the unemployed seemed downright heartless.

On February 26, 1931, he vetoed a bill that would have redeemed the bonuses promised to World War I veterans at fifty cents on the dollar. His reasons for vetoing the bill appeared petty to most veterans. According to him, payment of the bonuses would "benefit many veterans not actually in distress" and "upset the government economy." On July 11, 1932, Hoover vetoed the Wagner-Garner Bill, which would have extended the few federal relief efforts to the states, although he approved the Relief and Construction Act just a few weeks later. The bill authorized $1.5 billion in loans to state and local agencies for public works and provided for $300 million in temporary loans to states for relief programs. This was quickly followed by his approval of the Federal Home Loan Bank Act, which provided $125 million to banks, insurance companies and savings and loan associations for loans for construction of new homes—a measure that sought, in an off-handed way, to reduce unemployment.

Despite his slow movement toward a program of relief measures, Hoover faced a situation in July 1932 that would mark his administration forever with the label of being uncaring and unconcerned. Veterans, unsatisfied with Hoover's veto of the Bonus Bill in 1931 and the failure of the federal government to fully redeem their service vouchers, organized and moved to squat on Anacostia Flats. The first thousand arrived in late May 1932 and were subsequently joined by fifteen to sixteen thousand more. When Congress failed to approve a second Bonus Bill, the president ordered them to leave Washington. Although most of the veterans complied with the presidential order, some two thousand hardcore radicals remained. When an effort by the capital police resulted in the deaths of two policemen and two veterans, Hoover ordered Douglas MacArthur, who was the chief of staff of the army, to remove the remaining veterans. Using infantry, cavalry and tanks, the army expelled them, disregarding the fact that the shacks of the squatters contained not only male veterans but their families as well. The ugly specter of the army being ordered out against honorably discharged veterans forever tarnished the reputations of Hoover and MacArthur.

Although Hoover is generally regarded as the "No Deal" president, his approval of the Emergency Relief and Construction Act in July 1932 marked a change in direction and meant that the RFC had $300 million

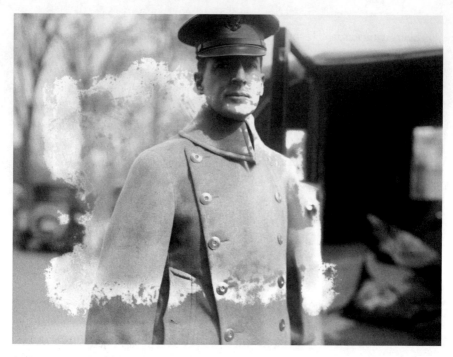

Douglas MacArthur, who would later serve as the army commander in the Pacific Theater during World War II, was responsible for clearing out the bonus army in Washington. His actions earned him the enmity of many veterans and were a blemish on his record of service to the United States. *Courtesy of the Library of Congress.*

more available to provide loans to states for relief. In Florida, Governor Doyle E. Carlton, who asked the Board of Social Welfare to carry out a survey to determine the extent relief was needed in the state, did not wait; he requested an initial loan of $500,000 to provide assistance to needy families. The first loan installment was received in September 1932, but it quickly became apparent that more money would be needed, and by the end of December, Florida had received almost $2 million in federal loans. Eventually, the amount lent to the state totaled $3.8 million before the RFC program was replaced in May 1933 by the Federal Emergency Relief Administration (FERA). During the ten months the Emergency Relief and Construction Act had been in operation, more than ninety thousand families in the Sunshine State had received assistance.

Despite Hoover's move to take some positive action to alleviate the suffering of Americans in the final year of his administration, for Floridians, it was too little too late. Although he had taken 59 percent of the popular vote in the election of 1928, his slow, confused and openly pro-business responses to the Depression made him an anathema to Sunshine State voters in 1932. The Republican rhetoric of "letting businessmen solve the economic problems" was no longer a viable idea for Floridians, who looked elsewhere for a savior.

Franklin Delano Roosevelt (FDR), the Democratic vice presidential candidate in 1928 and the incumbent governor of New York, partnered with John Nance Garner of Texas to carry the party's standard. Violating the tradition of awaiting formal notification of his selection as the Democratic candidate, FDR hurried to the convention to address the delegates and the nation. "I pledge you, I pledge myself to a New Deal for the American people," he promised, as he stressed the

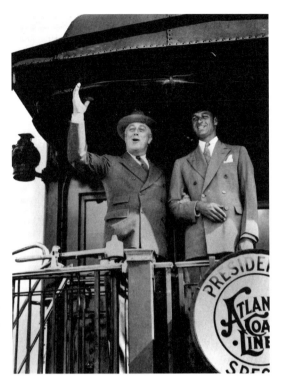

Franklin Delano Roosevelt, governor of New York and the Democratic vice presidential nominee in the election of 1928, brought new hope to millions of unemployed Americans when he promised a "New Deal" if elected president in 1932. *Courtesy of the Library of Congress.*

need for immediate and radical action to resolve the economic crisis.

Hoover, the reluctant Republican standard-bearer, ran a minimalist campaign, making few speeches and fewer appearances. His attacks on Roosevelt as a harbinger of radical change did little to change the minds of Americans who were ready for change. On October 31, just days before the election, he painted a dismal picture of what the proposed New Deal would do to the United States. According to Hoover, the New Deal would result in a nation where "the grass will grow in streets of a hundred cities, a thousand towns; the weeds will overrun the fields of millions of farms." "A lot of our neighbors," recalled Joseph Fink Jr. of Vero Beach, "went back North during the Depression. There was nothing here for them. They had to leave. They left their property, and the woods would catch fire and some of these places would burn." So how, asked many Americans, would Hoover's prediction of total ruin be any different from what had already happened?

Roosevelt conducted a vigorous campaign of train whistle stops and speeches. Sensing a landslide, state and local politicians rushed to join his crusade for change. In Florida, a usually solid Democratic state that had gone for Hoover in 1928, voters rejected several party stalwarts—including two former governors—and elected David Sholtz, a progressive graduate of Stetson Law School. Promising to actively seek help from the federal government and to implement reforms in education, larger expenditures for relief, jobs creation and stronger regulations of banks, Sholtz won the gubernatorial election by a two to one margin over his Republican challenger, William J. Howey. The 186,805 votes cast in his favor were more than any gubernatorial candidate had ever won.

Sholtz's victory meant that he had a Herculean task in front of him. In August 1949, Sholtz, writing to Edward C. Williamson of the University of Florida's History Department, recalled, "Certainly 1933 and 1934 were most trying years, for people were broke, hungry, desperate and many had lost faith. I shall never forget my first day in office to find, for the first time, actually that the State was not only approximately two million [dollars] in debt in its general fund operations, but actually had less than $5,000.00 in the fund. Yet with the credit cut off, as suppliers were demanding cash on delivery, we had approximately 9,000 people in the various State Institutions including the hospitals, who had to be fed three times a day, clothed and provided with a place to sleep, regardless of any other cost." Sholtz went to work immediately, getting the Sunshine State ready to receive the New Deal dollars that were sure to come.

On the national scene, FDR scored an impressive victory as well, winning 7 million more popular votes than Hoover and completely routing him in the Electoral College by a count of 472 votes to 59. In the Congress, Democrats won majorities in the Senate and the House of Representatives.

Florida and the nation were ready for change!

Chapter 11

"MAKE-WORK" PROGRAMS
ARRIVE IN THE
SUNSHINE STATE

*Our greatest primary task is to put people to work. This is no unsolvable problem
if we face it wisely and courageously. It can be accomplished in part by direct
recruiting by the Government itself, treating the task as we would treat the
emergency of a war, but at the same time, through this employment, accomplishing
greatly needed projects to stimulate and reorganize the use of our natural resources.*
—Franklin Delano Roosevelt, Inaugural Address, March 4, 1933

The New Deal had an immediate impact on the Sunshine State. Governor
David Sholtz, fresh from his landslide victory over William J. Howey,
immediately began to seek assistance from the myriad federal agencies that
seemed to spring up over night. In 1933, just before the expiration of the
FERA (soon to be replaced by another agency with the same initials), the
state received over $600,000, which was distributed to fifty-five counties to
pay the back salaries of some 4,500 teachers.

In August of that year, the first true New Deal agency—the Civilian
Conservation Corps (officially Emergency Conservation Work but
popularly referred to as the CCC)—to operate in the Sunshine State
began a reforestation program in the Olustee National Forest. The
program provided employment for 300 men, most of whom were white.
Within a few months, some 3,000 out-of-work Floridians were engaged
in similar projects in twenty-six camps around the state. Organized
along paramilitary lines, the CCC soon expanded its operations to
include the restoration of historical sites, the construction of camping

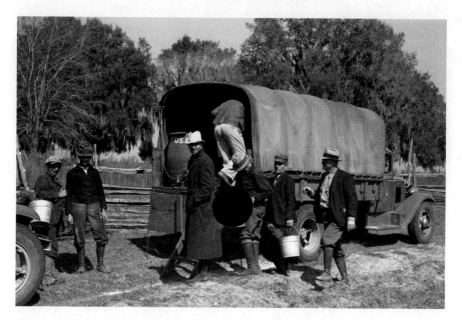

The Civilian Conservation Corps provided work for men, usually in the forest industries and in constructing parks. Here a group of CCC men get ready to plant trees in the Withlacoochee Forest in Hernando County. *Courtesy of the Library of Congress.*

facilities in state and national parks and other improvements. During the years the CCC operated in Florida (1933–1940), more than 40,000 young men cycled through the program, joined by an additional 2,500 administrators, teachers and skilled workers. Only men on relief were allowed to participate in the CCC program, and as a result, relief rolls swelled as men rushed to sign up in order to get into the organization.

The CCC workers were paid $30 a month and given free room and board and military-styled uniforms. Of their monthly salary, $25 went to their families and provided much-needed assistance to them. From April 1933 to February 1934, the three thousand CCC enrollees and their more than thirteen thousand dependents received a total of nearly $850,000 in wages. The average wage paid to CCC and other federal workers ranged from 30 cents an hour for basic laborers to more than $1 an hour for highly skilled craftsmen. Most of the workers (more than 53 percent) fell into the category of receiving forty to forty-nine cents an hour.

The agency amassed an enviable record during its existence, planting more than 13,000,000 trees, plowing 14,500 miles of firebreaks and improving 218,000 acres of forest stands. In addition, the CCC developed Highlands Hammock, Myakka River, Hillsborough River, Gold Head

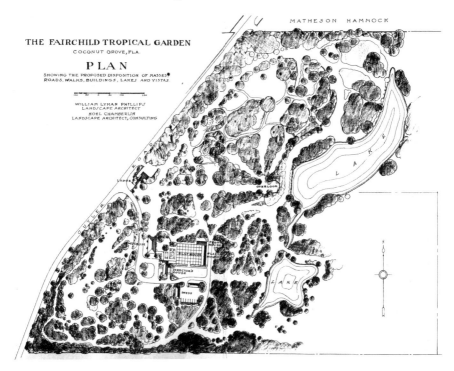

Fairchild Tropical Garden was a PWA project in Coconut Grove (Miami) and transformed an abandoned mining pit into a beautiful botanical garden. *Courtesy of Arva Parks McCabe.*

Branch, O'Leno and Torreya State Parks. The restoration of the pre–Civil War Fort Clinch in Fernandina Beach was also undertaken by the CCC, as was the development of the Florida Caverns in Marianna. (Today, the accomplishments of the CCC are on display at the Civilian Conservation Corps Museum at Highlands Hammock Park in Highlands County.) In Miami, the CCC transformed a former rock pit into Greynolds Park. It also built Fairchild Tropical Garden, another beautiful park.

The accomplishments of the CCC were tarnished by the agency's policies on including African Americans among the enrollees. The act that created the CCC in 1933 contained a clause stipulating that "in employing citizens for the purpose of this Act, no discrimination shall be made on account of race, color, and creed." Denied employment in jobs they had once dominated, blacks looked to the CCC for a source of work. Throughout the South, African Americans were denied enrollment in the organization, and since enrollment was predicated on need, states resorted to all kinds of dodges to avoid enlisting blacks in the CCC. In Georgia, for example,

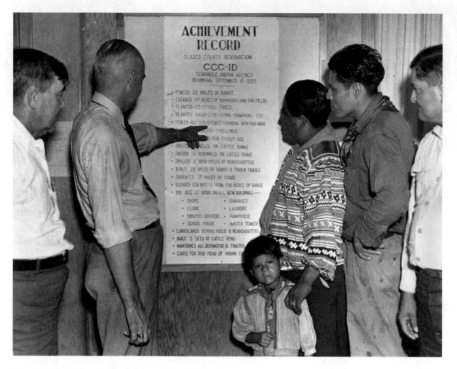

The CCC was organized along racial lines. Separate camps for African Americans and Native Americans were established, but these operated under the command of white army officers. Here a group of Seminoles review the group's progress with one of their supervisors. *Courtesy of the Patsy West Collection.*

the state legislature simply passed an act declaring that all Negroes were gainfully employed. When questioned about the lack of black enrollees, John de la Perriere, Georgia's CCC director, blandly declared, "At this time of the farming period in the State, it is vitally important that negroes [*sic*] remain in the counties for chopping cotton and for planting other produce. The negroes [*sic*] in this way are able to obtain work on the farms throughout the state." When pressed about the failure to enroll African Americans in counties that were more than 60 percent black, de la Perriere countered that the local county relief committees felt that "there are few negro [*sic*] families who…need an income as great as $25 a month in cash." In Florida, State Director John C. Huskisson, who had come to Tallahassee as Governor Sholtz's private secretary, reported, "On the basis of merit, no negroes [*sic*] have yet been selected for the CCC." Only after receiving a great deal of pressure from Secretary of Labor Frances Coralie Perkins and Director of the United States Employment Service W. Frank Persons, who threatened

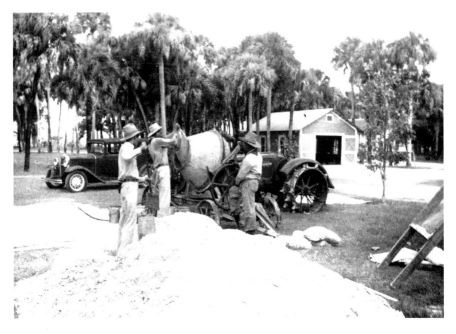

Seminole CCC workers mix concrete for a construction project on their reservation in the Everglades, circa 1935. *Courtesy of the Patsy West Collection.*

to remove Florida from the CCC program and cut off all funding, did Huskisson agree to "lower his standards" enough to accommodate 200 Negroes, though he refused to select them at the same depots as whites. Arkansas, Mississippi, Georgia—virtually all the southern states, plus northern states like Pennsylvania and New Jersey—attempted to subvert the racial equality provision of the enabling act. Interestingly, only Alabama's director tried to implement the provision, although he complained of the obstinacy of local selection boards in refusing to follow his instructions. Only the threat of funding losses seemed to have any impact at all on persuading southern states to enroll African Americans in the CCC. Eventually, some 200,000 African Americans found work through the CCC (out of a total of 2.5 million enrollees), but the bulk of these workers came after 1935 when whites left the organization for jobs in defense industries and other make-work programs. The failure of the Roosevelt administration to enforce the anti-discrimination clause of the enabling act left many blacks skeptical that any substantial changes in race relations in the United States would take place during the New Deal.

Even after they were enrolled, black workers in the organization were segregated into separate camps, denied access to supervisory jobs and kept under the command of white officers. Even the efforts of cabinet members like Secretary of the Interior Harold Ickes failed to bring about major changes. In 1935, he wrote the director of conservation works, Robert Fechner, "I have your letter of September 24 in which you express doubt as to the advisability of appointing Negro supervisory personnel in Negro CCC camps. For my part, I am quite certain that Negroes can function in supervisory capacities just as efficiently as can white men and I do not think that they should be discriminated against merely on account of their color. I can see no menace to the program that you are so efficiently carrying out in giving just and proper recognition to members of the Negro race."

The CCC was not different from most New Deal programs. The Roosevelt administration sought to retain the support of southern Democrats by tacitly abiding by local racial practices and prejudices, and this often meant saying one thing but doing another. The prejudice against blacks was not confined to the South, however, and the presence of a CCC camp composed of African Americans near a town or village anywhere in the United States was cause for complaints from local populations. Enrollment of Negro workers in the agency was limited, a policy that met with the silent approval of Roosevelt, for whom white votes were more important than improving the economic lot of African Americans.

On May 12, 1933, Congress approved the Agricultural Adjustment Act, which, among other things, established a subsidy program for the non-cultivation of crops like cotton and tobacco and the reduction of livestock herds. The idea was to bolster prices by reducing production. Unfortunately, the implementation of this program had the unintended consequence of putting thousands of tenant farmers and sharecroppers off farms and into the ranks of the unemployed. Although landowners benefited from the program by reducing operating expenses and rising prices, tenant farmers and sharecroppers were not so lucky. Many of them joined the great mass of the unemployed. By 1930, 81.3 percent of the state's inhabitants resided in cities or other incorporated communities.

Within the Agricultural Adjustment Act, which was directed through the Agricultural Adjustment Administration, was a provision that established the Land Policy Section (LPS) of the Division of Program Planning. Secretary of Agriculture Henry A. Wallace, a firm believer in government action in economic and social matters, was concerned about improving the lot of the rural poor and saw the LPS as a radical way to achieve this objective. The aim of the LPS was to find ways to take marginal land out of agricultural production, relocate the owners of this marginal land and find an alternative use for it. The vast expanses of such land in Florida made it a prime target for the LPS staff.

After a 1934 survey of sites in several southern states, the LPS selected Florida as a prime area for the creation of a land management pilot program. John Wallace, the brother of Secretary Henry Wallace, was among the survey group, and on January 9, 1935, he was named the project manager for what would ultimately become the Withlacoochee Land Use Project. After establishing his headquarters in Brooksville, John Wallace and his team of engineers, surveyors, foresters and lawyers began the task of acquiring land for the program, which became part of the Department of Agriculture's Resettlement Administration. Initial plans called for the purchase of 250,000 acres in Pasco, Hernando, Citrus and Sumter Counties in west central Florida, but two congressional budget revisions reduced the amount of money available so that Wallace was able to secure only 113,000 acres.

The selection of south Florida as the site of a Land Use Project was based on three factors. First, the area had a high rate of unemployment and economic distress. Within the four counties, more than 50 percent of the

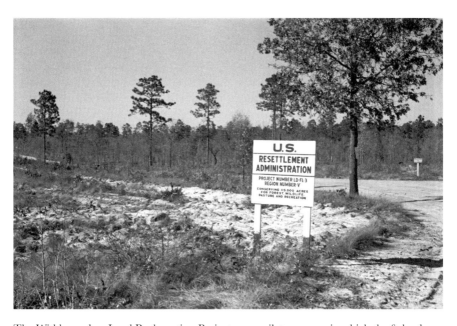

The Withlacoochee Land Reclamation Project was a pilot program in which the federal government bought abandoned or worn-out farmlands and converted them to forests. The Withlacoochee Project was a success, and today it is the Withlacoochee State Forest in Hernando County. *Courtesy of the Library of Congress.*

population was on some form of relief, and that rate was even higher within the actual project area. Of the thousands of acres targeted for acquisition, 95 percent was in the process of being foreclosed by state and county authorities for nonpayment of taxes. Federally purchased land would provide at least a modicum of financial relief for individuals and regional governments.

The second reason for selecting the Withlacoochee tract was the perceived opportunity for federal land use planners to develop and refine new techniques for land management, since the private owners had dramatically altered the environment of the area and upset the natural balance of the ecology of the region. Phosphate mining, cotton farming, truck farming and heavy timber cutting had depleted the soil fertility and had largely eliminated the habitats of wild animals, which upset the ecological balance of the targeted area. Withlacoochee would provide an ideal place to test ideas about land reclamation and restoration.

The third factor considered in the selection process was the proximity of Withlacoochee to the heavily populated areas of Tampa, St. Petersburg and Gainesville-Ocala, which had significant populations of unemployed workers. Once the LPS project got up and running, hundreds of individuals would be hired as laborers, which would help alleviate unemployment in

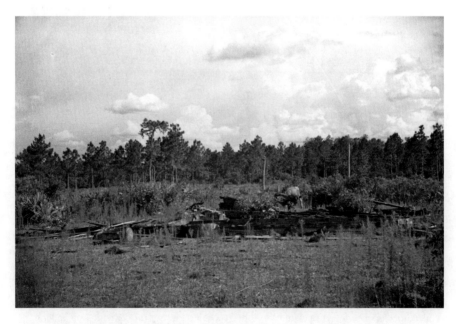

Abandoned lands within the Withlacoochee Land Reclamation Project were not suitable for farming, but they made excellent areas for newly planted pine forest. *Courtesy of the Library of Congress.*

the local communities. Once the land restoration project was complete, thousands would be able to take advantage of the newly rehabilitated lands and forests.

Even as the federal government was still acquiring acreage, in order to achieve the greatest results in the area, John Wallace and his staff were developing a model plan for other such projects. Within the four-county area, the LPS project (now referred to as the Withlacoochee Land Use Project) federal employees began an aggressive three-point effort—to restore the cut-over forest lands, to restock depleted or extinct native animal populations and to create public access areas for recreation and hunting.

In January 1936, a temporary tree nursery was established to furnish seedlings for the reforestation effort. By December of that year, over 330,000 slash and longleaf pine seedlings had been planted, and an additional 913,000 seedlings were planted by March 1937. To ensure that the young trees would survive, twenty-three thousand acres of land were cleared of competing oak and brush stands. To protect the new trees, John Wallace also supervised the construction of 357 miles of firebreaks and the erection of four fire towers, each one hundred feet high.

New Deal planners at Withlacoochee sought to improve land uses in other ways as well. In keeping with their plan of integrated land usage, Wallace and his subordinates seeded hundreds of acres of rangeland, and local cattlemen were authorized to continue their practice of open-range grazing. Cattle grazing produced secondary benefits of importance to the Withlacoochee experiment—cattle feeding on open ranges tended to reduce the hazards of forest fires by consuming patches of high grass and underbrush, and fattened cattle provided a source of revenue for their owners. The Withlacoochee planners sought to restore the depleted wildlife in the area by stocking herds of deer, flocks of turkeys and other game birds and by planting native food crops and special grain crops to sustain them. Abandoned phosphate mines, ponds and sinkholes were stocked with young fish, and in 1936 alone, more than seventy-five thousand bass fingerlings were released.

In cooperation with the Works Progress Administration, another public works agency, and the CCC, several recreation sites were developed in the Withlacoochee tact. Administrative facilities, cabins, pole shelters and other log buildings were constructed using the same "national park" style of architecture. The simple buildings could be easily erected by unskilled labor, and the materials needed could be gathered from the project area.

Keenly aware of the racist attitudes of white southerners in the 1930s, Withlacoochee planners constructed separate recreational facilities for

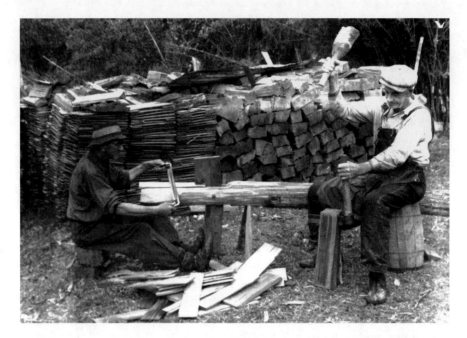

Within the Withlacoochee Land Reclamation Project acreage, CCC and WPA workers constructed a number of cabins, sheds and recreation areas to serve the surrounding population as parks. These two men are "riving" shingles to be used for roofing on the new buildings. *Courtesy of the Library of Congress.*

blacks. John Wallace's 1937 report on the progress of the Withlacoochee project noted the capitulation of the federal government to local folkways with only a single comment: "As there is a large negro population in some portions of the project area, one recreational development will be assigned to negroes for their use. This area will include picnic shelters and a baseball diamond."

The Withlacoochee land reclamation project had an enormous and immediate economic impact on Pasco, Citrus, Sumter and Hernando Counties. The purchases of land put money into the pockets of the small marginal landowners of the area and added much-needed revenue to the coffers of the counties as foreclosed-on land was bought by the federal government. The project also provided work for the unemployed in the adjacent areas. In December 1935, 166 men were on the payroll, and just four months later, that number had risen to 899. Although the number of workers had stabilized at around 500 by the end of 1936, federal administrators proudly pointed to the $261,000 that had been pumped into the local economy.

"Make-Work" Programs Arrive in the Sunshine State

The Withlacoochee Project was a model for other such projects around the nation. Development continued until the United States became involved in World War II and new uses for the land were found. The vast open areas of grazing pastures and the relative isolation of much of the land provided an excellent location for gunnery practice for pilot trainees of the U.S. Army Air Force. A firing range was established in the area near Dade City in Pasco County, and pilots from nearby airbases made regular runs to improve their combat proficiency. A control tower and makeshift tarpaper barracks were constructed on the Dade City range. Troops from the army's chemical warfare branch found another use for Withlacoochee. The heavy growth of some of the more remote parts of the project area approximated the jungle growth of contested islands in the Pacific theater of operations, and chemical defoliants were tested there before being used in combat. With the end of World War II, Withlacoochee returned to its primary mission. Within a few years after the end of the war, the entire site was transferred to Florida as the Withlacoochee State Forest.

The success of the CCC in Florida and the Withlacoochee Land Project spurred FDR's interest in another make-work project to pump relief funds into the Sunshine State. Since the earliest days of European occupation of Florida, dreamers had envisioned connecting the Gulf of Mexico with the Atlantic Ocean by way of a cross-peninsula canal. On September 2, 1935, Roosevelt revived this idea when he announced that, based on U.S. Army Corps of Engineers surveys, he wanted to proceed with digging such a canal and pledged $5 million in relief funds to do it. The announcement immediately touched off a round of vociferous protests from Floridians who thought a canal would ruin the state's freshwater aquifer by allowing saltwater intrusion to take place. Although the Corps of Engineers and state geologists declared that no saltwater intrusions would occur, they failed to convince most Floridians. Nevertheless, government agents began buying up land along the proposed route, and project directors constructed barracks for the anticipated horde of relief workers that would do the digging.

In his own administration, FDR faced considerable opposition. Secretary of the Interior Harold Ickes, who had responsibility for all public works projects, refused to approve the canal project for the Works Progress Administration. Ickes was not alone. In 1936, Congress refused to approve additional appropriations for the project once the initial allocation was used up, and it did so again in 1939. Despite the failure of FDR to get the canal completed as a New Deal project, proposals for such a canal continued to be put forth and some work continued sporadically until the Nixon administration cancelled the project in 1971.

Chapter 12
THE WPA

Everybody's working in this town and it's worrying me night and day
Everybody's working in this town and it's worrying me night and day
If that mean working too, have to work for the WPA.
— *Casey Bill Weldon, "WPA Blues," (1937)*

The largest of the New Deal agencies and a "make-work" organization that made a significant difference in putting the unemployed to work in Florida (and other states) was the Works Progress Administration (WPA). The WPA's purpose was to employ as many out-of-work Americans as possible, and to achieve this goal it developed several different sub-agencies to reach as many as possible. Americans became familiar with these sub-agencies— the National Youth Administration (NYA), Household Service Demonstration Project, Federal Art Project (FAP), Federal Music Project (FMP), Federal Theatre Project (FTP), Federal Writers' Project (FWP) and Historical Records Survey (HRS)—during the Depression years. Some, like the Household Service Demonstration Project, were aimed at teaching basic skills to unskilled workers, while others, like the FAP, FMP, FTP, FWP and HRS, were aimed at providing employment for white-collar workers who were not accustomed to performing manual labor. The NYA was designed to provide work for high school and college students so that they would not enter the job market and compete for work with unemployed men.

In addition to these activities, the WPA also had its own program for public works construction, which included such things as the construction of schools, building bridges, constructing community centers and parks, airports and erecting public buildings of all sorts. During its existence, the WPA (renamed the Works Project Administration in 1939 but retaining the same initials) spent a total of $13.4 billion carrying out these jobs. Many of the projects undertaken by the WPA were funded on a 70/30 percent basis, with state and local governments supplying the smallest amount (although the local government share sometimes fell to just 10 percent). Between 1934 and 1943, when the agency ceased to exist, more than eight million workers had been employed.

The WPA was the brainchild of Harry Hopkins, a social worker whose work with FDR in New York was considered revolutionary and successful. Hopkins was brought to Washington at the beginning of FDR's administration and given responsibility for overseeing the various relief programs of the New Deal. A firm believer in the philosophy that paid work was infinitely better than cash handouts, he set about creating programs that offered employment to virtually all segments of the unemployed population. Under the umbrella of the Federal Emergency Relief Administration and the Civil Works Administration, he created a structure for giving local governments grants to fund the construction of public works programs. Jobs on FERA projects were reserved for individuals who were receiving funds through direct relief. Employment on CWA projects was open to unemployed individuals, but the stipulation that workers be drawn from relief rolls was dropped. During its short lifespan, the CWA employed over four million workers, built 3,700 playgrounds, constructed 40,000 schools, paved 250,000 miles of highways and laid over twelve million feet of sewer pipe. In addition, the CWA built two hundred public swimming pools and a variety of other smaller projects.

While some critics were very vocal in their opposition to Hopkins's programs, particularly after 1935 when the CWA and FERA agencies were replaced by the Works Progress Administration, the WPA became the largest "make-work" program of the New Deal. Harold L. Ickes, who as secretary of the interior administered the Public Works Administration (PWA), feuded constantly with Hopkins. Still, Hopkins persisted with his idea of trying to take the millions on the relief rolls off the "dole" and put them to work. He defended his programs by saying, "Give a man a dole, and you save his body and destroy his spirit. Give him a job and you save both body and spirit." Throughout its existence, the WPA took over 90 percent of its workers from the relief rolls or from the ranks of the unemployed. Eventually, the WPA employed approximately 8.5 million people on some 1.4 million projects and pumped more than $13 billion into the economy.

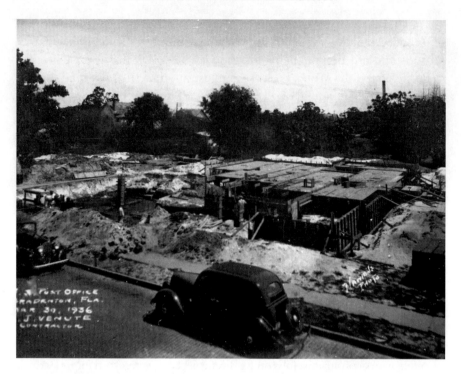

The WPA undertook the construction of numerous public buildings in the Sunshine State, many of which became post offices. In this photograph, WPA workers are seen building the foundation for a new post office in Bradenton. *Courtesy of the Manatee County Public Library System.*

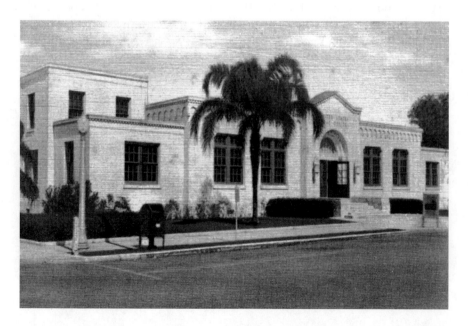

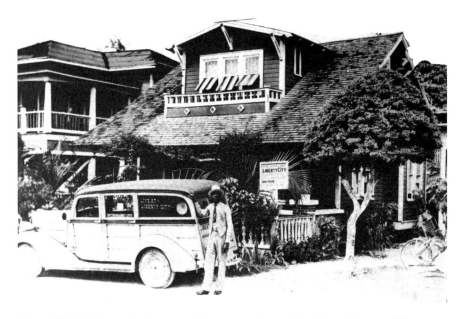

Alonzo "Pop" Kelly took advantage of the construction of the Liberty Square public housing project to develop his own Liberty City on land he had acquired years earlier. *Courtesy of Arva Park McCabe.*

Previous page, bottom: The new Bradenton post office in 1935. Many of these post offices have survived into the present and have been repurposed for municipal and not-for-profit organizations. *Courtesy of the Manatee County Public Library System.*

The public works record of the WPA during its seven-year history was impressive. Nationwide, the agency built over 125,000 public buildings, 2,500 hospitals, 1,000 airports and 124,000 bridges. It also paved over 650,000 miles of roads. In the Sunshine State, the list of WPA projects was substantial. In Miami, the WPA constructed two major public housing projects—Edison Courts for whites and Liberty Square for blacks—which provided low-cost housing for the city's poor. In Gilchrist County, the WPA built a new county courthouse in Trenton. In Tallahassee, a new Leon High School, three stories high, rose from the ground with an expenditure of $500,000 by the WPA. In Sarasota, the WPA granted the city $131,000 to build a bay front park and a municipal auditorium. When the facility opened in February 1937, more than three thousand people attended the opening celebration.

One of the most grandiose buildings erected by the WPA was the Federal Court House in Tallahassee. Designed by New York architect Eric Kebbon in the Beaux Arts and Neoclassical styles, the building cost $318,000 and was completed in 1936. Because the building also housed a post office on the first floor, the lobby was decorated with eight murals depicting scenes from Florida history—all the work of Hungarian-born artist Edward Buk Ulreich. Although it has been remodeled several times, great care has been taken to retain the original architectural features and Ulreich's murals. The courthouse is now occupied by the U.S. Bankruptcy Court of the Northern District of Florida.

In 1936, Daytona Beach received a grant of $184,000 from the WPA, which it matched with $84,000 in city funds to transform a run-down section of beachfront into a community-use band shell and boardwalk. Opened in 1937, the facility could seat 4,500 persons and was used for outdoor concerts and community events. It is still in use today and is one of the most prominent landmarks in the city. In west Tampa, George Nelson Benjamin, a developer and mayor, donated land for a public park that became the eventual site for Fort Homer Hesterly Armory. In 1922, the City of Tampa and Hillsborough County donated the land to the Florida National Guard. Construction of the armory began in 1938. The federal government, under the Work Projects Administration, contributed $361,880. The armory was completed in 1941, dedicated on December 8, 1941 (the day after the attack on Pearl Harbor), and served the 116th Field Artillery Battalion of the National Guard. Palm Beach also boasted an armory built by the WPA. Designed by the noted architect William Manley King, the old armory building is still in use as the Robert and Mary Montgomery Art Center.

Vero Beach saw its airport improved and runways lengthened by the WPA, while the Martin County Courthouse was enlarged and modernized. On Davis Islands in Tampa, the WPA built the Peter O. Knight Airport, which served as the city's main airport until 1945, when it took over Drew Field, a U.S. Army Air Force facility. The $462,264 spent on constructing the Knight Airport included a seven-panel painting depicting the history of aviation by George Snow Hill, a minor regional artist. The paintings are now on display at Tampa International Airport. Throughout the Sunshine State, in hundreds of small villages and towns, the WPA constructed airports and landing strips. Although these projects were considered essential for progress during the 1930s, their real value did not become apparent until after 1941, when most of them were taken over by the army and navy for use in training pilots for the war effort.

Tampa not only received WPA funds to build its airport—between 1933 and 1941, the city and the surrounding unincorporated county would

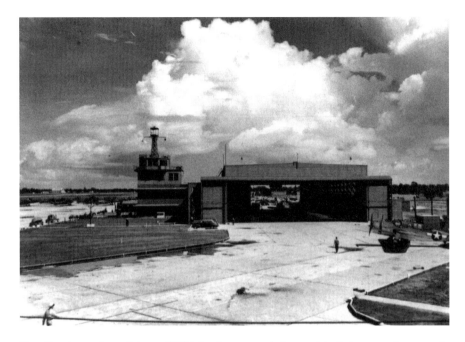

Vero Beach was the recipient of WPA funds to upgrade its municipal airport and to extend its runways. When war came in 1941, the airport became the Vero Beach Naval Air Station. *Courtesy of the Wynne Collection.*

eventually receive a total of around $19,800,00 in federal funds. In 1935, the WPA and the Public Works Administration provided the resources necessary to once again reconstruct the Bayshore Boulevard in Tampa into a 6.5-mile-long continuous sidewalk—the longest in the world—at a total cost of $1.2 million. In addition to this restoration and renovation project, the WPA spent nearly $1 million on renovating and expanding the facilities at the Tampa Bay Hotel, which the city had acquired in 1905 from the estate of Henry Plant. Repairs to the hotel cost $138,000; another $186,000 went for the development of Plant Park; $129,000 for grandstands and bleachers at Plant Field; and $465,000 for buildings and other improvements at the fairgrounds. Of the almost $20 million spent in Tampa and Hillsborough County, $4 million were contributed by the city government (by private citizens and various companies) and through donations of land and materials. WPA officials estimated that almost $15 million had been spent on labor costs alone. Without the wages paid by the WPA, Tampa would have been mired more deeply in the Depression. In October 1935, the WPA reported 3,675 workers on its rolls. This figure jumped to 5,032 by January 1936.

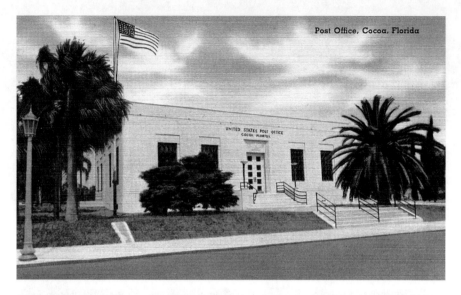

The small city of Cocoa opened its WPA-built post office in 1939. After years of service as a post office and a federal office building, it was purchased in 1999 by the Florida Historical Society for use as a library and headquarters building. *Courtesy of the Florida Historical Society Post Card Collection.*

Florida saw the construction of more than one hundred post offices by the WPA during the heyday of its operations. Utilizing an architectural style sometimes referred as "Depression Deco" and in some cases utilizing plans that had been used in other places, the agency replaced smaller, often ramshackle buildings with state-of-the-art concrete and stone structures, many of which are still in existence. In Arcadia, for example, the WPA-built post office has a twin in Cocoa that has been converted into the headquarters of the Florida Historical Society. Some of the more ornate and substantial post offices, particularly those with murals created by unemployed artists through the WPA-sponsored Federal One program (which eventually employed over forty thousand out-of-work artists nationwide), have become points of local pride. The Arcadia post office has a unique plaster sculpture above the postmaster's door inside the lobby that was completed in 1939 by Constance Ortmeyer.

Elsewhere around the state, the WPA took on projects of all sizes. While some of these might not seem important today, they were considered important in the Depression—and they provided work for the unemployed. In St. Augustine, the historic Government House was enlarged and remodeled for use as a post office. In Newberry, the agency built a municipal building; in San Antonio, it constructed a city hall; Greenville also got a city hall and jail, courtesy of the WPA; and Jupiter saw the construction of a wooden civic center. Fort Myers was the beneficiary of two major WPA projects, Lee Memorial Hospital and a yacht basin. Union County relocated and renovated its old courthouse and replaced it with a new one at a cost of $39,000, paid from WPA funds. Lake Worth secured a new post office—and the list goes on.

In Woodsmere, near Orlando, the WPA built a tuberculosis sanitarium for the "care of about 350 patients including 90 negroes [*sic*]." Jefferson County got a new jail; the University of Florida saw a new student union building completed; St. Petersburg Junior College got a new campus; and Orlando could boast a new football stadium, courtesy of the WPA. In Tampa, the Clara Frye Hospital was built by the WPA for black patients in 1938. Toney Coral Gables welcomed the WPA and received two new buildings in exchange. On February 15, 1937, the Coral Gables Woman's Club and Library opened, followed in 1939 by the Coral Gables Public Safety Building.

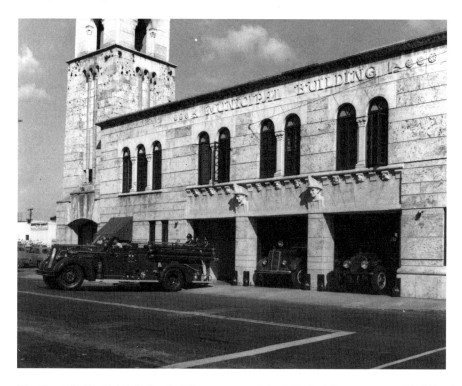

The Coral Gables Public Safety Building was one of the WPA buildings constructed in Miami during the Depression. It was large enough to house three fire trucks at one time. *Courtesy of Arva Parks McCabe.*

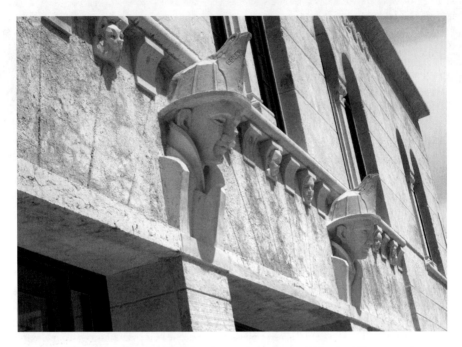

The Coral Gables Public Safety Building featured cast busts of idealized firemen on its façade, quite a fancy touch for such a building. *Courtesy of Arva Parks McCabe.*

Critics, particularly political opponents of FDR, thought money spent on WPA projects was wasted on the undeserving and merely served to create a vast political machine to secure his reelection. These complaints reached such a fever point that Congress passed the Hatch Act in 1939 to prohibit politicking by WPA staff and employees. Others complained that the WPA promoted communism or that work carried out by the agency was overpriced. Many of the complaints were due to the fact that different areas of the nation received approval for projects and funding at different levels. Although FDR had referred to the South as the nation's "number one economic problem," the region received only 25 percent of WPA funding on a per capita basis. Those who saw the fine hand of politics in every agency action pointed to the fact that the South was solidly Democratic and would vote for FDR anyway but other regions needed to be bought with federal funding. Still, the criticism continued.

Much of the criticism leveled against the agency had to do with the perception that the lack of strict supervision encouraged workers to develop poor work habits and to waste money by shirking hard work. The WPA and its workers were ridiculed as being lazy, and the agency's initials were said to stand for "We Poke Along," "We Piddle Around," "We Putter Along,"

The WPA

"Working Piss Ants" or the "Whistle, Piss and Argue gang." Comedians poked fun at the WPA, and the stereotype of several workers with shovels standing around while one man dug a hole was commonplace. In the South, where kudzu was planted by WPA workers to curb soil erosion, the standard joke was that the plant grew so fast and the workers moved so slow that the lumps a passerby saw in kudzu-covered fields were workers who did not move fast enough to get out of the way of the growing plant.

Perhaps the strangest WPA project in the state came when the agency bought fifteen thousand acres in Madison County and relocated five hundred families from Miami, Jacksonville and Tampa there in 1935. The Cherry Lake Rehabilitation Project was an experiment in communal living. A sawmill and lumberyard, a cane mill and a cooperative store were built by WPA workers, who also erected 170 cottages for the families to live in. The self-contained village also included a new school, an auditorium and barracks. Lawrence Westbrook, the New Deal bureaucrat who directed the Rural Rehabilitation Division of the FERA, considered Cherry Lake and other such communities in Arkansas and Georgia to be laboratories for developing ways to end farm tenancy and sharecropping in rural areas. According to him, the projects functioned "as independent rural foundations devoting their resources to the development of patterns of living for the share-croppers and farm workers without capital, who would otherwise be indefinitely on relief."

In rural Okaloosa County, the Resettlement Administration developed Escambia Farms, another model farm project, which included homes, schools, community buildings and a store. Eighty-one homes were built on 115 tracts of land. In addition to financing the purchase of land and farming equipment for poor farmers and sharecroppers, the Resettlement Administration also built migrant camps to provide workers with clean housing and facilities at low rent. Like the earlier Withlacoochee project in Hernando County, the Resettlement Administration undertook environmental projects dealing with soil erosion, water pollution and reforestation. World War II marked the end of the Farm Security Administration, and funding was drastically reduced during 1942 and 1943. The program was officially abolished in 1946 when the Farmers Home Administration (FHA) Act replaced it. The FHA provided direct loans to qualified buyers, and the idea of cooperative communities was abandoned. Escambia Farms School, however, continued to operate under the control of the Okaloosa County School Board until 1963. The community commissary was operated as a general store for many years by several local families.

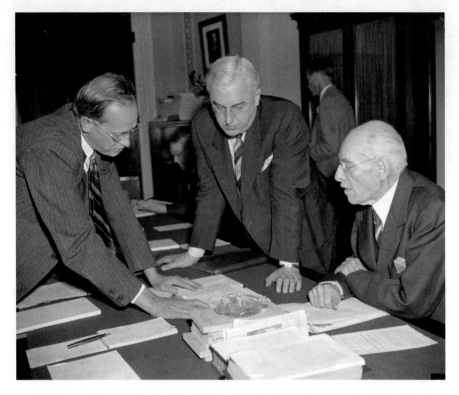

Harry L. Hopkins, head of most of the New Deal make-work programs, explains the workings of the various programs to members of Congress in 1938. *Courtesy of the Library of Congress.*

Despite their initial successes, Cherry Lake, Escambia Farms and other similar projects made little difference in the lives of the masses of the rural poor in Florida.

Harry L. Hopkins, who directed the WPA, was willing to take on virtually any project as long as it took people off the unemployment rolls and put them to work, even if this meant infringing on activities of other New Deal agencies. His battles with Harold Ickes, the secretary of the interior, were epic, but Hopkins persisted successfully with the full backing of FDR and Eleanor Roosevelt. He was so influential with the Roosevelts that FDR retained him as a special advisor and diplomatic troubleshooter after the dismantling of the WPA.

Chapter 13

THE "HARD TO EMPLOY" AND WPA PROJECTS

Few things could add such a permanent volume of employment as would a program of educating the public to use the services and participate in the pleasures of the culture we possess. I use the word culture as including everything from basketball to a violin performance.
—*Harry L. Hopkins,* Spending to Save *(1936)*

You would have had to decide about 560,000 white-collar men. Would you make them suffer? Would you put them out in a ditch with a pick axe and make them like it, musicians, actors? We decided to take the skills of these people wherever we found them and put them to work to save their skills when the public wanted them. Sure we put musicians into orchestras. Sure we let artists paint.
—*Harry L. Hopkins, address at a WPA luncheon (September 19, 1936)*

One of the most vexing problems for Harry Hopkins when he assumed responsibility for taking out-of-work Americans off the relief rolls and putting them to work was the question of how to treat those who were not normally considered part of the labor force. White-collar workers, professional musicians, artists, writers, actors, directors and even high school and college students did not fit easily into the skilled and unskilled masses of manual laborers. They belonged to special classes of specialists, and Hopkins realized they needed to be given special tasks. When members of his staff protested the inclusion of such individuals on the WPA rolls, Hopkins is reputed to have scotched dissent with the simple declaration, "Hell, they

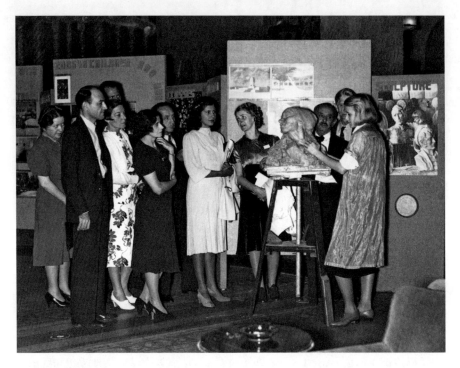

Sculptor Joan Keller demonstrates her technique for creating a bust in clay to this group of interested Manatee County citizens. She, like hundreds of other artisans, was employed in the Federal One program, better known as the Federal Art Project. Artists such as Keller provided artwork for WPA buildings, post offices and public buildings. *Courtesy of the Manatee County Public Library System.*

have got to eat just like other people." Even before the creation of the WPA in 1935, while directing its predecessors FERA and CWA, he had taken steps to provide for these "unemployables" by granting $1.8 million to the Treasury Department to create works of art in public buildings such as post offices. Some 3,600 artists in all forty-eight states produced more than forty thousand pieces of art—murals, sculptures and other works—in a program known as the Public Works of Art Project. When the FERA and CWA were phased out and replaced by the WPA, employment of individuals from this segment of the population continued under the Federal One program, which was expanded to include more people. Initially under the direction of Jacob Baker, whose tenure lasted less than a year, Federal One was the umbrella organization for the WPA's relief efforts in the arts.

Holger Cahill, an Icelandic immigrant and former acting director of the Museum of Modern Art, was a journalist and expert on American folk art. He had attended Columbia University and The New School for Social

Research and was appointed the director of the Federal One program to succeed Baker. He soon expanded the program to include the Federal Writers' Project, the Federal Music Project, the Federal Theatre Project and the Historical Records Survey. At the peak of its existence, the Federal One program including all the sub-agencies—provided work for more than forty thousand individual artisans. Each of the arts projects had a national director, a regional staff, a state director and a local administrator. Cahill's first love, however, was the original Federal Art Project.

By March 1936, the FAP was firmly established in the hierarchy of federal agencies and counted more than six thousand artists on its rolls. About three thousand of the enrollees were actively engaged in creating works of art, while approximately fifteen hundred were engaged in art education. The remaining FAP workers were engaged in art research, photography and other auxiliary projects. The scope of artistic works produced by the FAP included murals, sculptures, silk-screen prints, posters for various other agencies and photographs and cover designs for federal publications, especially those produced by the Federal Writers' Project.

By 1938, forty-two thousand easel paintings and eleven hundred murals in public buildings were commissioned. Today, FAP-created art is considered a community plus and is often considered a tourist "draw." Art education, another FAP undertaking, was promoted through the establishment of hundreds of community art centers that served tens of thousands and sponsored hundreds of individual and group exhibitions. Many of the art centers are still functioning today. Another of the FAP's major activities was the creation of the Index of American Design, which helped popularize American folk art by documenting the country's "usable past." Some twenty thousand photographic records of American art, painting, sculpture, handicraft and folk art were made, resulting in the largest single source of materials about the history and evolution of art genres in the United States. With the outbreak of war in 1941, the FAP contributed to America's war effort by producing thousands of posters, which served as propaganda to raise the spirits of the American people, for factories, recruiting stations and government buildings.

Just as artists had to eat, so too did musicians. The Federal Music Project, which became the largest of the four WPA "projects" and employed more than sixteen thousand workers, was led throughout most of its existence by Russian-born Nickolai Sokoloff, a violin virtuoso in his youth and the conductor of the Cleveland Symphony Orchestra. The FMP operated in all forty-eight states and was administered by state and regional directors.

Dr. John Nice of Jacksonville was the Florida director of the FMP, and he divided the state into five smaller areas centered in Tampa, Pensacola, Miami, Orlando and Jacksonville. Each of the smaller regions had its own administrator and went its own way musically. Three times a year, the Florida FMP staged musical festivals in various locations around the state, including DeFuniak Springs, Tallahassee and Miami. Orchestras from around the state would give combined performances, sometimes to celebrate special occasions and to mark the openings of new federal projects such as the opening of the Federal Art Galleries in Miami. Generally, however, the distances and difficulties involved in transporting musicians and equipment from other Florida regions to Miami limited their appearances in that city. The Miami orchestra was disbanded in 1937 because the city could support only one orchestra and the University of Miami had an existing orchestra that the FMP did not want to compete with. A smaller orchestral group called the New Miami Federal Orchestra was formed in 1938.

In Jacksonville, the Florida Symphony Orchestra (FSO) was placed under the direction of Dr. John Bitter, the former dean of the University of Miami's School of Music. The FSO was extremely popular and appeared at different locations in the northern half of the Sunshine State. Federal funding was often inadequate to pay the traveling expenses of the symphony, so small admission charges were imposed (one dollar for full admission, ten cents for standing room) for concerts. Local civic, cultural and social organizations also sponsored orchestra appearances, advancing travel funds and selling tickets. In St. Augustine, the FSO appeared under the auspices of the Junior Service League, while the Eustis Music Club sponsored a concert in Eustis. The Ocala Choral Society and the Primary Parent-Teachers Association co-sponsored the FSO in that city. When no larger venues were available, the FSO presented its programs in high school auditoriums and churches. Sometimes spaces were so small that a smaller version of the FSO presented the program.

The FMP used a number of volunteer and paid guest conductors to lead the symphonies. On January 14, 1938, the *Daytona Beach Morning-Journal* proudly announced that the FMP national director, Nickolai Sokoloff, would be conducting the Jacksonville Symphony Orchestra in that city as part of a FSO tour of Miami, St. Petersburg and Hollywood, Florida. Touring brought a lot of attention for the FMP orchestras. On October 16, 1936, the *Florida Flambeau*, the student newspaper of the Florida State College for Women in Tallahassee (FSCW), featured a long article on the two-day musical festival to be held on campus on October 21 and 22. It followed a two-day festival in Jacksonville and marked the start of a statewide tour. The highlight of the Tallahassee event was to be a performance of Verdi's "Aida" by the combined orchestral choruses from Tampa, Miami and Jacksonville. Where possible, the FMP orchestras worked with existing municipal and collegial symphonies, and Florida was fortunate to have college orchestras at Stetson College, Rollins College, the University of Florida, the University of Miami and, of course, FSCW.

In Tampa, the FMP established a community chorus and an orchestra, and in Ybor City a Latin Opera Company was formed. The Latin opera depended on hiring foreign singers, and after the House

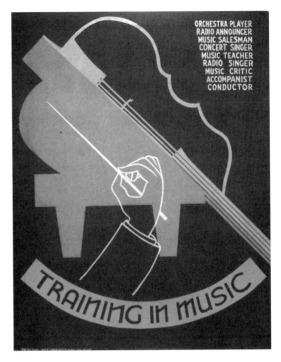

ORCHESTRA PLAYER
RADIO ANNOUNCER
MUSIC SALESMAN
CONCERT SINGER
MUSIC TEACHER
RADIO SINGER
MUSIC CRITIC
ACCOMPANIST
CONDUCTOR

TRAINING IN MUSIC

The Federal Music Project put on numerous public performances and carried out extensive music education programs in cities and towns throughout Florida. Although no posters advertising such activities in the Sunshine State are available, this one from Ohio serves to give an idea of the scope of these educational programs. *Courtesy of the Library of Congress.*

Un-American Activities Committee under Texas congressman Martin Dies protested, it was disbanded. In addition to the Tampa orchestra, the FMP established an orchestra in St. Petersburg, but the lack of skilled musicians on the WPA rolls and the costs involved in hiring professionals away from paying jobs played havoc with its funding. In 1937, the orchestras in Tampa, Jacksonville, St. Petersburg and Miami were consolidated into a single touring symphony known as the Florida Federal Symphony Orchestra.

The FMP in Florida was involved in much more than creating and maintaining orchestras. It conducted a massive music education program for the public (particularly in rural schools), reduced relief rolls by hiring copyists to hand copy printed musical scores (although it would have been cheaper to simply purchase printed copies) and hired teachers to give music lessons to groups and individuals. By 1937, the FMP reported that more than twenty thousand lessons had been given in public schools alone. In addition, the FMP hired teachers to direct choruses, bands, ensembles and amateur community productions and group sings. Roving performing units were kept busy giving performances in schools, community centers, orphanages, prisons, hospitals, public parks and rented halls in urban and rural areas. The Federal Music Project began in July 1935 and ended in 1939. The FMP was among the most popular of WPA programs, and to placate public outrage at its demise, it was replaced by the WPA Music Program, which lasted from 1939 until 1943—by which time it had been pressed in war service on the homefront.

In 1935, Harry Hopkins selected Hallie Flanagan, the director of the Vassar College Experimental Theatre, to create the Federal Theatre Project, a network of regional and municipal theater companies. Flanagan set to work with a will, eventually fielding a staff of 7,500 unemployed actors, directors and technicians to produce original plays and the works of established playwrights like Sinclair Lewis and Eugene O'Neill. The FTP was among the most controversial of all the WPA cultural projects, eliciting the condemnation of the Dies Committee, but it was also the only WPA unit to turn a profit—an estimated $2 million during its four-year existence. The aim of the FTP, said one official, was "to stress not only new American plays based on the history of each region, but also classical material appropriate to each locality." According to a FTP press release, the "purpose and duty of the Theatre [is] not only to entertain, but to inform the people"; however, "the Federal Theatre does not take sides in any controversy be it social, political, or otherwise."

That might have been the aim of the FTP, but reality was something else. Directors of the various units argued forcefully for independence in selecting productions and often went their own way. The Yiddish Theater Project, for example, presented *Day Is Darkness*—which was advertised as the famous anti-Nazi play by George Fress—and took it on tour to places as far away as Boyle Heights, California. The Negro Theater Project in New York featured *Turpentine*, a dark play about the life of African Americans in the turpentine camps of northern Florida. Written by Augustus J. Smith and Peter Morrell, the play sparked little interest among the white downtown public, who preferred Negro performances that catered to their perspective of African Americans as "exotic." The *Amsterdam News*, on the other hand, reported that "plain working people and their problems were movingly dramatized." The Seattle Negro unit produced *Stevedore*, another play about working African Americans; but by and large, in the early days of the project the Negro units confined themselves to the classics, musicals, folk plays and melodrama, a fact due in part at least to white directorial control in most units and to the paucity of scripts written by Negro playwrights. None of these groups faced much in the way of condemnations or reprimands from the FTP administrators on the national level.

FTP units existed in Tampa, Miami and Jacksonville, with touring groups that frequently took productions to Orlando, St. Petersburg, Tallahassee and Pensacola. In addition, small theatrical units at Florida's private and public colleges received support from the FTP, as did small community playhouse groups. The most unique FTP unit in Florida was the Hispanic Theater, housed in the Centro Asturiano Club in Tampa. The only

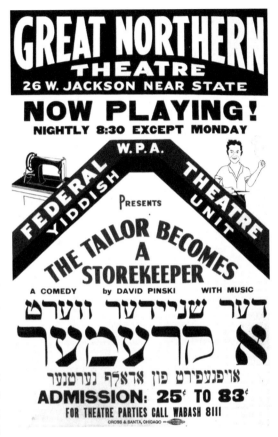

David Pinski was a favorite playwright for the Yiddish Theater in New York. This poster advertises his play *The Tailor Becomes a Storekeeper*, which also toured in several nearby states. *Courtesy of the Library of Congress.*

Hispanic unit in the nation, it operated side by side with an Anglo-America unit and produced its own repertoire of plays, although occasionally the two units came together to present works that were well received. On July 28, 1937, the *St. Petersburg Times* carried an article that listed the various productions for both companies that year. Tampa also had a fully functioning Negro Theater, which built on a strong theatrical history among black residents of the city. A third unit, the Tampa Vaudeville Theater, occasionally used Hispanic actors integrated into its otherwise all-white cast but remained in Tampa proper.

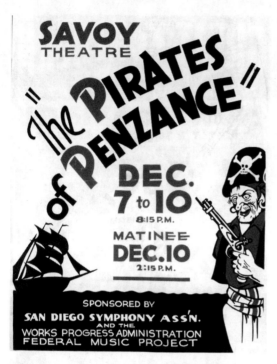

Units of the WPA's Federal Theatre Project often presented the same plays on a loosely coordinated national schedule, but just as often, local unit directors selected their own plays, which were usually tailored to fit the tastes of local audiences. *Courtesy of the Library of Congress.*

The Miami Federal Theater was also very active, producing a number of plays written by local playwrights. One play, *Sand in Your Shoes*, was based on Ponce de Leon's discovery of Florida and was produced in Tampa and Jacksonville. Marjorie Stoneman Douglas authored several one-act plays for the Miami troupe, including *The Gallows Gate*, about an argument between a mother and father regarding the character of their son who is sentenced to hang. Among the other productions by the Miami theater group were special plays written to celebrate their city's ties with Latin and South America, including short plays about Bernardo O'Higgins and Simon Bolivar. A favorite production was *Rhapsody in Two Flats*, a play by Edgar Hay. So too was the comedic farce *Boy Meets Girl*.

The Jacksonville Federal Theater (JFT) went its own way as well. From May 13 until June 1, 1937, for example, the JFT featured *One More Spring*, adapted from the Robert Nathan novel by Lulie Hard McKinley. *Miles Glorious*, a modern translation of a Roman comedy, was one of the plays the JFT toured to various high schools and small auditoriums in surrounding towns in 1937. So too was David Belasco's *Girl of the Golden West*, which debuted in April 1938. From serious dramas to comedic farces, such as the three-act play *Engaged*, the Jacksonville Federal Theater tapped into the local communities and provided cheap quality entertainment.

In cooperation with mandates from the national headquarters, the Florida units presented certain productions that Flanagan thought promoted patriotic values—although the FTP proclaimed its neutrality. One such play was *It*

Can't Happen Here, adapted by Sinclair Lewis from his novel of the same name. The national staff of the FTP envisioned a simultaneous opening of the play in FTP units in twenty-two separate venues. On October 27, 1936, Lewis's *It Can't Happen Here* opened across the country. Interestingly, the FTP national staff tried to depoliticize the play by sending all units instructions to avoid "all controversial issues—political angles of any degree—special appeals—racial or group appeals—or inferences in any of these directions, since Federal Theatre is interested only in presenting good theatre, neither adapting nor assuming any viewpoint beyond presenting a new and vital drama of our times, emerging from the social and economic forces of the day. Also forbidden in most positive terms are any references to any foreign power, any policy of a foreign power, the personalities of any foreign power or government; any comparison between the United States and any specific foreign power, system, personality, etc." FTP units immediately violated this prohibition, and the Yiddish Theater Project in New York used Germany as the setting for its production. The Federal Negro Theater in Seattle also took great liberties with the setting and dialogue, casting whites in the roles involving the few town citizens who were fascist sympathizers while the rest of the townspeople were black. Dorothea Lynch, the first Florida director of the FTP, hastily commissioned a Spanish version of the play for use by the Hispanic group. It was an unmitigated disaster, since the form and dialogue of the play did not translate well into the language or traditional forms of Hispanic theater.

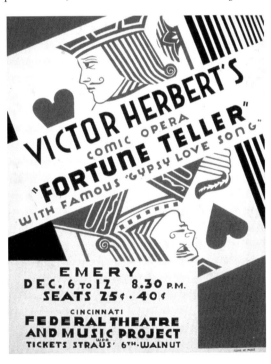

The Tampa Hispanic theater group was both a source of pride and trauma for the national WTP

Since the working actors in the Federal Theatre, Dance and Music Projects were unemployed professionals, many unit directors offered well-known classics, such as Victor Herbert's opera *Fortune Teller*. This allowed the actors to demonstrate the range of their talents. *Courtesy of the Library of Congress.*

officials. It was the only Spanish-language WPA theater unit in the nation—this elicited a great deal of pride, but given the tendency of Ybor City residents to get actively involved in political causes (which were reflected in the selection of plays), it was also a matter of grave concern. Under the direction of leading man Manuel Aparicio, the unit often presented plays that reflected the biases of Latinos against Spanish General Francisco Franco and his fascists and their strong feelings for the Spanish Republic. The Spanish revolution was a politically charged issue that drew strong comments from conservative American politicians that viewed support for the republic as support for communism. Conservative political hackles were raised even higher when it was discovered that a large percentage of the group's actors were foreigners who had not applied for citizenship.

In 1937, Congress made significant changes in the wording of the Emergency Relief Appropriation Act, which funded the WPA and the FTP. Twenty-five actors, including director Manuel Aparicio, were dismissed. Other members,

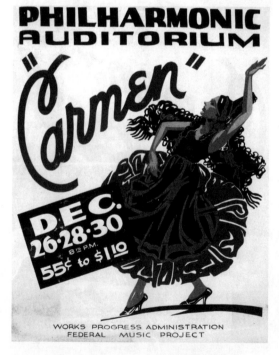

For some productions, units of the Federal Theatre Project joined with units from the Federal Music Project and the Federal Dance Project to present more complicated stage offerings, such as the comic opera *Carmen. Courtesy of the Library of Congress.*

such as native-born Chela Martinez, were fired because their family income was too high to qualify for relief. Francisco Fernández Rey, the president of the Centro Espanol, made a fervent plea to Florida State Director Frank Ingram, who had replaced Lynch as the state director, and argued against the dismissal of the troupe members. He reminded Ingram that the "majority of Latin Actors who are being laid off are men and women who have lived many years in the United States, making the United States their home, obeying its laws, paying taxes, raising families, and the majority of them have American-born children to support who would suffer privations and even hunger were their parents to be left permanently without employment." There was nothing to be done, and the Hispanic theater closed after fourteen shows and forty-two performances, which were viewed by more than twenty-three thousand spectators. By the end of 1939, the Federal Theatre Project was closed down entirely. The Florida Federal Theatre Project had delivered nine hundred performances to an estimated audience of four million.

Within the Federal Theatre Project was the Federal Dance Project, a WPA project created to provide employment for dancers and choreographers. It too was under the direction of Hallie Flanagan and had units in New York, Chicago, Los Angeles, Philadelphia, Tampa and Portland. The Tampa unit, which concentrated on teaching dance and staging presentations in ballet, modern dance and vaudeville, featured directors Senia Salomonoff, Asa Thornton and Josef Castle. Like the theatrical units of the FTP, the dancers in the FDP were encouraged to develop dances that portrayed local condition without making political statements of any kind. Unlike its bigger brother, the FDP remained largely out of the controversies that plagued the FTP.

The last of the WPA cultural agencies was the Federal Writers' Project, which was particularly active in the Sunshine State and continues to have an impact on the study of the state today.

Chapter 14
THE FEDERAL WRITERS' PROJECT

Only such a set-up as a WPA Writers' Project could compile so thoroughgoing a treatise on an entire state [Florida] as is this latest addition to the American Guide Series. The added achievement of being not only exhaustive, but largely interesting, fresh, authoritative, and at moments even entertaining, is unique for a guidebook.
—The Saturday Review of Literature, *1939*

The Federal Writers' Project was conceived by New Deal administrators as part of Federal One, the common name for the four WPA arts programs. After it was created in 1935, the FWP provided jobs for unemployed editors, writers and research workers. Directed by Henry G. Alsberg, the author of *America Fights the Depression* (1934), the FWP operated in all the American states and eventually employed some 6,600 men and women in 1938. A total of more than 20,000 writers and researchers passed through the agency before it was de-funded by Congress in 1939. The FWP was the federal government's answer to finding work for individuals whose professions did not easily fit into the mainstream of the WPA's "make-work" programs. It too came under criticism from conservatives as being "communistic" and "elitist," and Alsberg wound up defending his agency in front of the Dies Committee on Un-American Activities in December 1938. During its four-year existence, the FWP created units that dealt with history, travel, architecture, ethnic studies and folklore. It produced more than one thousand pamphlets and books, including the well-received American Guide series and the American Slave Narratives.

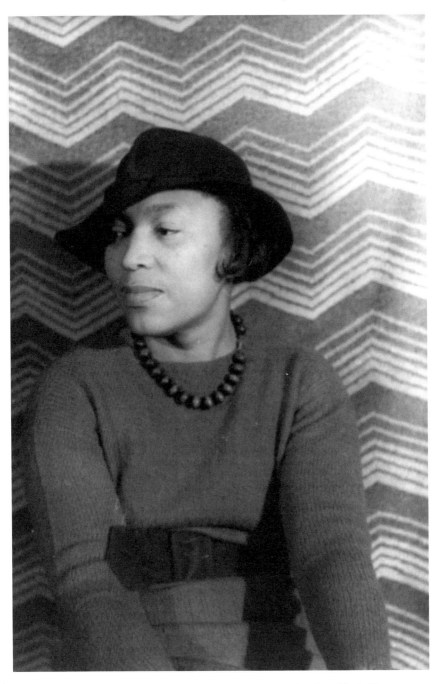

Although she was a published author and a noted anthropologist, Zora Neale Hurston was unemployed in 1938 and on relief. She joined the Federal Writers' Project and went throughout Florida collecting African American folk tales and folk songs. *Courtesy of the Library of Congress.*

Employees of the FWP worked for prevailing wages in the state, and this varied. Workers in New York and other urban venues earned considerably more ($93.50 to $103.50 per month) than their counterparts in rural states like Georgia, Mississippi and Florida, where monthly wages were as low as $39 a month. Supervisors and editors earned more. Stetson Kennedy, an editorial supervisor and field interviewer in Florida, earned $75 a month. Zora Neale Hurston, a published author, joined the Florida FWP in 1938 as a "relief writer" assigned to work with the FWP's Negro Unit. Initially paid $67.50, she was ultimately given a $75 travel allotment that raised her salary to $142.50 per month. The average monthly salary for unskilled workers in the FWP was $20 a month, although it was gradually increased.

Carita Doggett Corse of Jacksonville was appointed head of the Florida FWP unit. Corse, who had published two books on Florida history, was paid $2,500 a year, a princely sum for the 1930s. Corse had little administrative experience, and it showed as she tried to get the Florida FWP up and running. Eventually, the unit undertook a multitude of tasks, ranging from the mundane typing of copies of published books to innovative projects involving interviews of the state's population of former slaves—a project she credited as being the brainchild of Hurston.

During the four-year life of the Florida FWP, the number of persons employed varied from one hundred to two hundred, and they were scattered across the state in offices in Gainesville, Jacksonville, Lakeland, Miami, Orlando, Pensacola, St. Augustine, Key West, St. Petersburg and Tampa. The largest of the offices was in Jacksonville, which also served as the operating headquarters for the state's Negro Unit. The Negro Unit, housed in Clara White Mission in Jacksonville, was composed originally of ten members, but subsequent budget cuts reduced the number to three by December 1936. Martin Richardson, Alfred Farrell, Viola Muse, James Johnson, Paul Diggs and Rachel Austin were the principal writers for most of the life tenure of the unit. Hurston was added in 1938. The Negro Unit produced a manuscript, "The Florida Negro," written primarily by Martin Richardson and edited by Stetson Kennedy, but a sponsor to publish the project could not be found. A minor controversy persists among scholars about how much of a contribution Zora Neale Hurston actually made to the manuscript. Robert Hemenway, Hurston's biographer, maintains that she contributed heavily, while Gary McDonogh, who published the work in 1993, maintains that her contributions were no more than other writers and that Richardson should rightly be acknowledged as the author.

Florida had an unusually large number of unemployed white writers, since many of them had previously been employed as publicists during the land boom of the 1920s. In addition, many rural newspapers in the state could no longer afford to publish and closed their doors, leaving writers/reporters out of work. With the exception of administrative personnel, the FWP writers had all been on relief when hired and welcomed the chance to practice their profession for modest salaries. Most were glad to have jobs, but Hurston, the acknowledged star of the group, was shamed by having to work for the FWP in order to get off relief and never made any public acknowledgement of working for the agency. Other published authors like Rolland Phillips (a detective story writer), Albert Manucy (a historian who directed the Key West unit) and Carl Lester Liddle (writer for *Danger Trails* magazine) freely acknowledged their association with the FWP. For Stetson Kennedy, who would become a published author after the demise of the FWP, working for the agency was the defining moment in his life.

The FWP's primary goal was the compilation and publication of the American Guide Series, a collection of travel guides that featured individual states, and a total of thirteen guides were produced and printed. Given the increasing popularity of travel by automobiles and the rapid spread of highways across the nation, the guides not only provided work for writers but also documented historical information about specific places and peoples. The manuscript for the Florida book, *Florida: A Guide to the Southernmost State*, was pored over by Henry Alsberg's staff in Washington, and some passages were removed as being "too salacious" and "too detrimental" for publication. One passage concerned the location of a red-light district in Tampa and was taken out. The Florida guide was paternalistic and condescending to African Americans in tone, reflecting the southern view on race, although contributors and editors tried to inject a more liberal tone to the text, which again triggered epic battles at the state and national level. Describing the battles fought over the material, Stetson Kennedy noted that "they won some and we won some, so it is fairly well balanced."

The Florida guide was the first in the FWP's series and was six hundred pages long with photographs and maps. The photographs were produced in collaboration with the Farm Security Administration (FSA), although some local Sunshine State photographers like Gleason Waite Romer of Miami also made important contributions. Published by Oxford University Press, the Florida guide set high standards for other state units to meet.

Combining the Florida WPA's Folklore Project with the Negro Unit resulted in a number of original recordings of songs and interviews and included Lebanese immigrants in Miami, Greek residents of Tarpon Springs, white lower-class farmers and African Americans. On May 23, 1939, Corse sent a letter to Henry Alsberg, the national director, noting Hurston's contribution: "The enclosed 'Proposed Recording Expedition Into the Floridas' was written by Zora Neale Hurston, Negro editor of the Florida Project. I believe that Zora can assist the expedition in getting…excellent and original recordings in the State. If possible, she should accompany the expedition on its trip through Florida, as she has an intimate knowledge of folk song and folklore sources in the State." She, along with Stetson Kennedy and folklorist Alan Lomax, carried wire recorders to such out-of-the-way places as isolated turpentine camps in north Florida to the homes of Bahamian immigrant bean pickers in Belle Glade. Hurston quickly established camaraderie with African Americans, but oftentimes it was necessary for Kennedy and Lomax (both white) to intercede with white employers and property owners to get permission to record. Utilizing the skills she had learned while studying with Franz Boas at Columbia University, Hurston, along with Kennedy, collected scores of personal histories, including interviews with former slaves, which were revealing about race relations in the Jim Crow South. Copies of the personal histories are held in several libraries in Florida and represent a fertile field of scholarship since they have not yet been published as a single volume.

There was another, though less-known, New Deal cultural agency that operated in the Sunshine State. Originally part of the FWP, the Historical Records Survey was split off as a separate agency in 1936 under the direction of Luther Evans. Using unemployed clerks, teachers, librarians and archivists, its principal job was to copy and catalog records of all kinds: state records, church records, county records—even records of graveyard burials. In addition, the HRS undertook the job of collating congressional votes, indexing unnumbered executive orders and identifying and collating collections of presidential papers and messages. The HRS was financially the most efficient of all the Federal One/WPA programs and averaged 2,500 employees a month (with a high of 6,000 employed in 1938) at an average salary of $73 per month. With the end of the WPA cultural programs in August 1939, Luther Evans resigned. New director Sargent Child took over, but congressional budget cuts continued. The program continued to function as part of the Community Service Program, but by 1941, the central staff was reduced to only 12 employees. The HRS papers for the Sunshine State are most often catalogued today as part of the Federal Writers' Project papers.

An overall assessment of the work of the Florida Writers' Project and the HRS is that they produced a great deal of new and innovative work. More than any of the other New Deal cultural agencies, the Florida branches gave a good return on federal dollars.

Chapter 15

THE NEW DEAL
AND MINORITIES

*I believe the days of letting people live in misery, of being rock-bottom destitute,
of children being hungry, of moralizing about rugged individualism in the light
of modern facts—I believe those days are over in America. They have gone, and
we are going forward in full belief that our economic system does not have to force
people to live in miserable squalor in dirty houses, half fed, half clothed, and
lacking decent medical care.*
—*Harry L. Hopkins,* Spending to Save *(1936)*

*I want you to help me…would you please write just a few lines to the W.P.A. and
tell them to give me work at the sewing room so I can make a honest living for my
children. Please mam write me a few lines so I can present it to the W.P.A. office.*
—*Annie Klee Dixon to Eleanor Roosevelt, March 22, 1939*

Nearly 15 percent of all WPA workers were women. Despite its much-proclaimed goal to take everyone off relief rolls, the agency reflected the prevailing belief of the time that a woman's proper role was that of a housewife. The employment of women was further restricted because officials felt that hiring more than one person from a single family would limit the jobs available to other breadwinners from other families. Although statistics for the Sunshine State are not readily available, national studies revealed that approximately 90 percent of the WPA-employed women were single, widowed, divorced or had been deserted by their spouses. Mixed in with these categories were spouses of men who were handicapped, disabled or too old to work. Some areas did have WPA projects that were aimed primarily at hiring women. In Arcadia, the agency built sewing rooms where women were taught to use sewing machines and employed to make clothing, bedding, mattresses and other items for use in hospitals, adoption centers and orphanages. In Tampa, beginning in 1935 and continuing until 1943, between 1,200 and 1,450 women operated sewing machines at sixteen different locations in the city, many of which were vacant cigar factories. Throughout the state, small sewing rooms were established—in Madison, Crystal River, Jacksonville, Lakeland, Hallandale and just about every town, large and small. Although the wages were small, it was often the only income a family might have. More than six thousand sewing rooms were in operation nationwide, employing 150,000 women.

Some women were employed in clerical or secretarial work for the WPA, but the number was small when compared to the number of men hired for construction work. A few, like Carita Doggett Corse, who headed up the WPA Federal Writers' Project in Florida, were given administrative positions. Women with special homemaking skills were sometimes hired for jobs with the Household Service Demonstration Projects, which taught the region's poor new techniques in meal preparation, childcare and other household skills. Other women found work as nurses, teachers, librarians and cafeteria workers. The number of female WPA workers was restricted somewhat by the agency rule against more than one WPA job per household, a rule that many Florida women protested as not being realistic because of fluid family circumstances. Elna C. Green's remarkable *Looking for the New Deal: Florida Women's Letters during the Great Depression* captures the anguish and despair of women who found themselves shut out of gainful employment by this rule.

At the March 1936 Democratic Women's Regional Conference for Southeastern States, Ellen S. Woodward, assistant administrator in charge of women's activities, addressed a conference of women in Tampa and put forth an optimistic view of what the WPA was doing for unemployed females:

> *I wonder whether the women in this country, and men too, realize just what the creation of the Women's Division in such a program signifies. It means the Administration is determined that women shall receive their fair share of work and that it has made special provision for the enforcement of that policy. When the President said that no able-bodied citizens were to be allowed to deteriorate on relief but must be given jobs, he meant women as well as men. Harry L. Hopkins, our Federal Administrator, has*

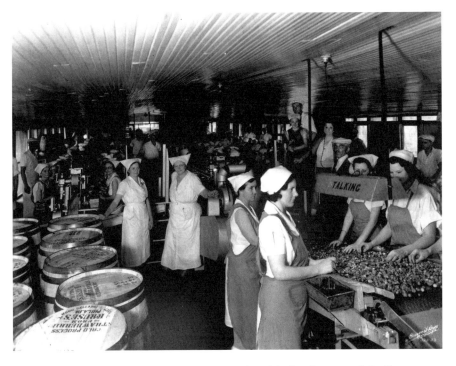

Women constituted a large segment of the unemployed during the years of the Great Depression. Mostly unskilled, women found work in canning factories and sewing rooms, both of which provided some jobs under the WPA. *Courtesy of the Library of Congress.*

repeatedly stated that "needy women shall receive equal consideration with needy men." As evidence that this policy is being carried cut, there was a study made about six or eight months ago, end it was found that at that time fifty-three percent of all the men who were eligible for work were working, and that fifty-three percent of all the women eligible for work were also working. At this particular time in the new program, approximately sixty-five percent of the employable women are now at work, and new projects are rapidly being put into operation to take care of the additional number who are eligible.

Although Woodward's words were all positive, they failed to take into consideration the discontent among women workers that bubbled beneath the surface. Women frequently complained that wages paid to them were less than those paid to men (the WPA's policy was to pay slightly less than the prevailing private wage). WPA officials had little statistical data on which to base their wage scale for women, and disparities certainly existed. So

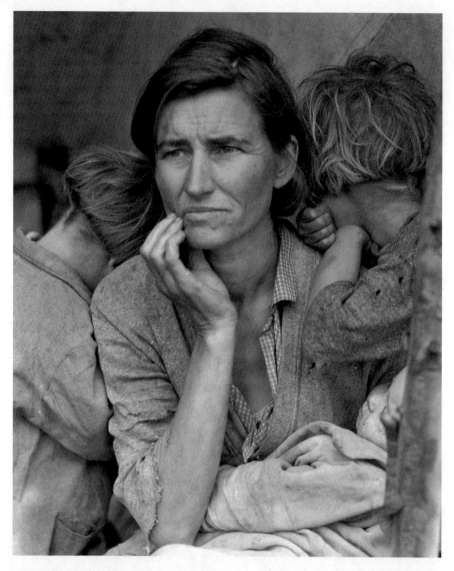

Women found it difficult to find regular employment in the 1930s, and the bulk of WPA jobs required physical labor beyond their capacities in most cases. As a result, most women stayed home to care for their children while men worked on government jobs. *Courtesy of the Library of Congress*.

few women were in the workforce before the onset of the Depression that reliable data was impossible to gather. Other complaints focused on the "favoritism" certain women were supposedly given by friends or relatives on the local relief boards that selected workers for WPA employment. It was a common complaint, and certainly such favoritism existed, although not on a widespread basis. Other complaints centered on the fact that local WPA funding was sometimes delayed by officials in Washington. (A three-week delay in the distribution of WPA paychecks had produced a small riot in Tampa on September 7, 1935, when four hundred disgruntled workers clashed with police.) Even when funding arrived in time to meet payrolls, it was occasionally insufficient to continue the employment of all workers. Class differences were also a bone of contention, and female workers frequently complained that middle- and upper-class "society girls" were awarded cushy jobs for which they had no experience, while more deserving and experienced women were forced to take menial jobs that made no use of their skills. Some women complained that others were given jobs although they did not meet the relief "means" criteria.

Dissatisfaction with the WPA and the perceived mistreatment of women reached the boiling point in Tampa on July 8, 1937, when a group of about one hundred women employed in a WPA sewing room in Ybor City went on strike. Ybor City, a cigar manufacturing section of Tampa, had a long and violent history of labor troubles and strikes, and the city was home to a number of radical groups that sought to recruit dissident workers into socialist, fascist or communist groups. City officials had sometimes used the authority of local law enforcement agencies to break up strikes and often ignored the illegal actions of anti-strike vigilantes. Although the women were federal employees and although they were engaged in a nonviolent protest, city officials and many whites were appalled that they had the temerity to strike. In the *Tampa Tribune*, opponents and supporters wrote letters to the editor. One writer gave his opinion that the "sewing room project is merely a modified form of direct relief. Practically none of the women employed on this project are qualified workers. Many of them have never been employed prior to the opening of the sewing room projects. However, as these women all have dependents and are entitled to relief, we feel that the proper solution would be to give them direct relief so that they could stay at home with their dependents, where they are needed."

Although the strike attracted the support of the Tampa branch of the radical Workers' Alliance, it was doomed from the beginning. Only about one-quarter of the 400 workers at the Ybor City facility participated in the strike. Mostly Latinos, they failed to gain the support of their white and black co-workers who continued to work during the labor stoppage. Support also failed to materialize from all but approximately 250 male workers from the 3,700 men working on the thirty-nine other WPA projects underway in the county. Finally, after four days, the striking women abandoned their protest.

The strike was a complete failure, producing no changes at all in the sewing room conditions, no increase in wages and no changes in WPA administrative personnel. The leader of the strikers, Mable Hagen, a member of the Workers' Alliance, lost her job and was forced to return to the relief rolls once again. The Workers' Alliance gradually faded into obscurity, hampered by charges that it was a communist organization.

Two months after the strike, the WPA changed its eligibility rules, excluding non-citizens from working for the agency. Many of the Latin women working in the Ybor City sewing room lost their jobs because many of them, while living in the United States most of their lives, had never taken steps to acquire citizenship. In addition, many Latin men from the area also lost their WPA jobs, throwing entire families back on relief rolls and sending disgruntled workers into the arms of radical organizations.

Chapter 16

FLORIDA AND THE "BIG BILL"

Dad worked for the Works Progress Administration, building roads and parks during the Depression. In those struggling times, it was the only work he could get...I always said if I could work as hard as my dad, I'd have no problem making it in this world. Dad left for work before sunrise, and he'd come home after sunset. When the WPA experience was over, he became a driver for companies that delivered bread, laundry and meat.
—Jim Otto, Hall of Fame football player, 1999

In June 1933, Congress passed the National Industrial Recovery Act (NIRA), which included the Federal Emergency Administration of Public Works—more popularly known by its later name, the Public Works Administration (PWA). Under the direction of Secretary of the Interior Harold L. Ickes, this agency was unique for the time because its purpose was to stimulate the economy through large-scale spending on construction projects such as dams, bridges, highways, schools and hospitals. With a two-year budget of $3.3 billion, the PWA created projects and farmed them out to private contracting firms, which did the actual designing, hiring and building. The original objective was to construct projects that were too big and expensive to be undertaken by a single community or state. By the end of its life, however, the PWA had achieved both its objectives—it had contributed to the revival of the American economy and had dramatically improved and expanded the nation's infrastructure. Among the major projects of the PWA were the Grand Coulee Dam, the completion of the Hoover Dam, the contribution of funds to the Tennessee Valley Authority and the construction of the Muscle Shoals electrification project and countless other projects in cooperation with the CCC and the WPA.

The PWA was set up to become a funding program, utilizing the so-called multiplier effect—that is, to make funds available to private contractors for approved public works, who would then provide jobs for the unemployed and pump money into the local economy through purchases of materials and supplies. The funding carried two controversial stipulations—contractors had to recognize labor unions and they had to hire African Americans, which they did although blacks were usually employed for the most menial tasks. By June 1934, the agency had distributed its entire fund to 13,266 federal projects and 2,407 non-federal projects. For every worker on a PWA project, it was estimated that two additional workers were employed in providing materials and services needed to complete the project. During its lifetime, the PWA consumed roughly one-half of the concrete and one-third of the steel produced in the United States.

Florida was among the earliest states to benefit from the infusion of money from the New Deal and the PWA. In 1934, the city government of Key West was bankrupt. Throughout the 1920s, the city's population had decreased and its financial resources declined. By 1933, the city's accumulated debt was more than $5 million, it was behind on bond interest payments to the tune of $250,000 and there were no funds in its treasury to meet current obligations. In a dramatic move, city officials asked Governor David Sholtz to declare a state of emergency so that the city, which had long been a key naval port, could be turned over to the federal government for rescue. The rehabilitation of Key West was the kind of high-profile project New Deal planners were looking for to demonstrate their new approach to solving the nation's economic woes.

With a lot of cash and the talents of city planners, the federal government set out to make Key West a tourist destination, and early results seemed to confirm the government's decision. An estimated forty thousand visitors came to Key West by the end of 1934, but the Labor Day hurricane of 1935 destroyed the city's vital Overseas Railroad connection and brought the economic revival to a momentary halt. The hurricane also killed almost three hundred persons, including forty-four World War I veterans who were in three CCC camps working on the construction of a highway to connect the city with the mainland. Although the hurricane represented a serious setback for redevelopment efforts, the highway opened in 1938 and provided a new lifeline for the city. With the outbreak of World War II, Key West's fortunes received a boost when the naval station was expanded to accommodate blimps, ships and airplanes.

Key West was not the only PWA project in the Sunshine State. Approximately six and a half miles of the famous Bayshore Boulevard in Tampa, popularly claimed to be the longest continuous sidewalk in the world, were completely renovated and expanded. In addition to such projects as this, the PWA also was involved in constructing new buildings on the campuses of the state's universities and colleges. In 1938, the PWA completed a new infirmary on the campus of the Florida State College for Women in Tallahassee. Under the leadership of John J. Tigert, the University of Florida received funding for several new buildings as well. Elsewhere, PWA projects in the Sunshine State included

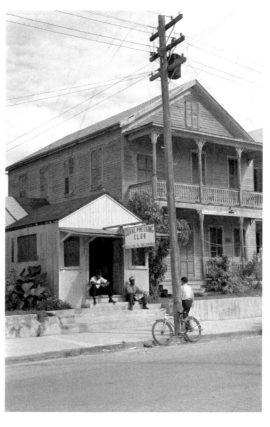

In 1934, Key West officials declared the city was bankrupt and turned responsibility for operating the town to the federal government. Using the city as a demonstration project in urban revitalization, the federal government sent in the WPA, city planners and tons of money to make the town—which had languished after the First World War—into a thriving tourist destination. *Courtesy of the Library of Congress.*

public housing in Liberty City (Miami), Orlando and Tampa. Over its lifetime, the PWA constructed more than twenty-nine thousand public housing units nationwide. Even such mundane tasks as building privies in Oviedo were funded by the PWA. In Ocala, the Florida Industrial School for Girls was a PWA project. Throughout Florida, the PWA also funded the expansion, improvement and construction of more than one hundred airfields. These projects would prove invaluable to the American war effort after 1941.

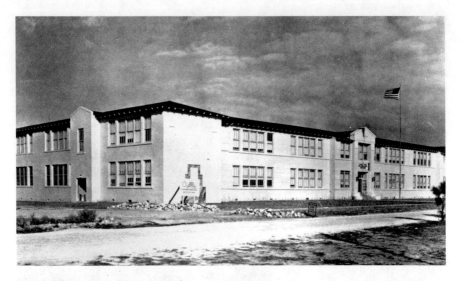

Coral Way Elementary School was built by the PWA in Miami, as were several other municipal buildings and the Miami Shores Elementary School. *Courtesy of Arva Parks McCabe.*

The PWA often worked with the WPA to fund and build projects. In Pensacola, the two agencies combined resources to build new high schools for the city's white and black populations. Miami was the recipient of a number of PWA projects. With federal funds allotted to the PWA, the "Magic City" witnessed a building program that saw the city acquire several new public buildings, including the Miami Beach Post Office, the Coral Gables Woman's Club, the Miami Shores Golf Club and the Coral Gables Municipal Building. In addition, the PWA was responsible for adding a new building to the campus of Jackson Memorial Hospital, as well as three public schools—Shenandoah Junior High School, Coral Way Elementary School and North Beach Elementary School.

With war clouds gathering in Europe and Asia, the Roosevelt administration was concerned about the closure of American shipyards and the failure of industry to replace the aging ships in the merchant marine fleet of the United States. The situation was critical as the administration began to slowly prepare for a war that was sure to come. In 1935, Congress enacted the Merchant Marine Act, which funded the construction of ten merchant ships a year for ten years. For American shipyards, which had constructed only two dry cargo vessels between 1922 and 1935, the Merchant Marine Act was a godsend. Not only did it provide a market for new ships but it also featured a "no lose" cost-plus incentive for builders and operators.

Florida and the "Big Bill"

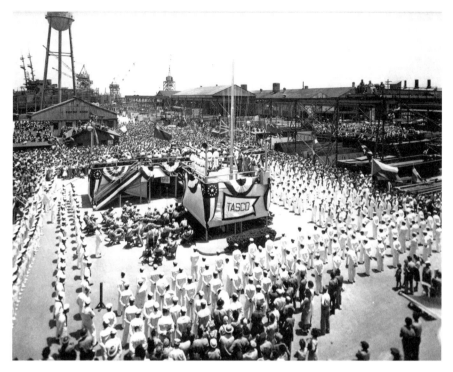

The Tampa Shipyards (TASCO) were initially opened on the strength of federally guaranteed contracts on a cost-plus basis and with a PWA loan. The original owner, Ernest Kreher, was forced to declare bankruptcy, and the firm was taken over by Tampa banker George B. Howell. Howell operated the shipyards successfully until the end of World War II. In this picture, TASCO executives receive the navy's highest award for achievement. *Courtesy of the Library of Congress.*

In Tampa, Ernest Kreher secured a PWA loan, built a large dry dock and, in 1939, was given a contract for $8 million to construct four cargo ships. The contract was a godsend for the city, since the shipyard immediately employed some 2,000 workers—fully one-third of the 6,400 unemployed men in Tampa. However, the good news didn't last. After the completion of a single ship, the *Seawitch*, Kreher announced that the company was in serious financial difficulty and would not be able to complete the contract. The Maritime Commission and the Reconstruction Finance Corporation, which had assumed the PWA loan, looked around for new management. George B. Howell, a local banker, stepped in and purchased the company for $500 and assumed its debts. Under Howell's leadership, Tampa Shipyards continued operations until 1946, producing over three hundred small freighters and employing more than 12,000 men and women by 1943. By 1945, three major shipyards operated in Tampa.

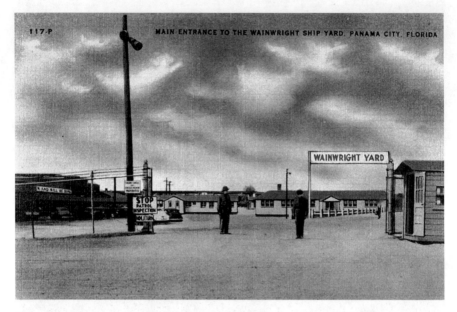

The Wainwright Shipyard in Panama City was Florida's largest and most productive shipyard and was also constructed with PWA funds. The yard closed at the end of World War II. *Courtesy of Bay County Public Library.*

By 1941, the Sunshine State could boast additional shipyards in Miami, Jacksonville, Panama City, Pensacola, Orlando and Dunedin. Most of these yards received initial contracts from the PWA and the Maritime Commission and produced ships of all sizes, from freighters and tugs to Liberty ships and amphibious vessels.

The PWA played a vital role in the modernization and expansion of the United States' military facilities prior to 1941. Although most American politicians believed that Europe would soon be enveloped in a new war, American isolationists controlled a considerable bloc of votes in the Congress and were less than willing to actively spend money on military preparedness, despite the repeated calls for increased funding by the nation's military chiefs. Roosevelt, who had first recognized that the United States was woefully unprepared for the possible war when he authorized the Maritime Act of 1936, realized that it would be easier to channel funding for upgrading old bases and creating new ones through the PWA. As a result, the PWA was given sole responsibility for allocating money for projects designated as essential by the military. Once again, Florida benefited from these expenditures.

In 1939, Brigadier General Vivian B. Collins, the adjutant general of the Florida National Guard, had chosen a 27,000-acre tract in Clay County to

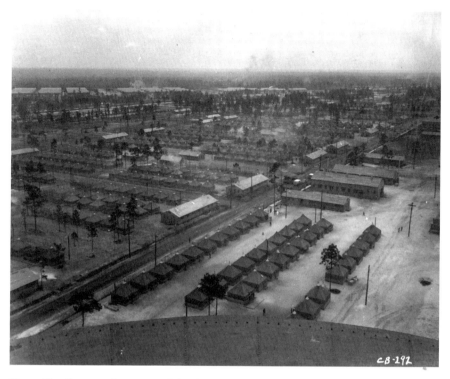

Camp Blanding, a major army training base in Clay County, was constructed in a very short period (just months) as PWA, WPA and CCC workers were used to construct the necessary buildings and training ranges. *Courtesy of the Wynne Collection.*

replace Camp Foster, a guard reservation transferred to the navy. Florida, which had also received a payment of $400,000 from the federal government, planned to build a training base there for its infantry units. When the military planners began looking around for new bases to house the projected 1,200,000 troops and 800,000 reserves who would be called up for training under the proposed Selective Training and Service Act of 1940, the new base was considered an ideal location. Eventually, the army would lease an additional 150,000 adjacent acres and process more than 1,000,000 men through training at the facility.

In a complicated arrangement, some $28 million in funding for the development of the base (now named Camp Blanding, after General Alfred Hazen Blanding) was committed to pay for the work. Routed through private contractors, who did their own hiring, and the WPA and CCC, which drew laborers from the relief rolls, some ten thousand permanent and temporary buildings were erected in less than a year. From swamps and forests emerged the fourth-largest city in the Sunshine State.

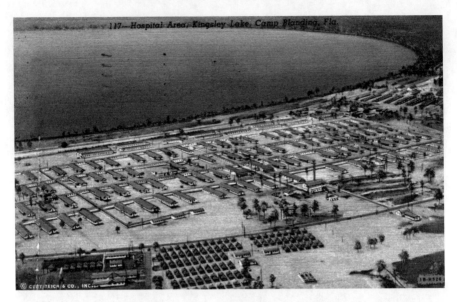

By 1943, Camp Blanding had become the fourth-largest city in the Sunshine State. More than 1.5 million draftees were trained in this single army base. The base hospital was the largest and most active in Florida. *Courtesy of the Wynne Collection.*

While the army was busy in Clay County, the U.S. Army Air Force (AAF) was busy elsewhere. In 1938, Hillsborough County had donated some 5,700 acres of land to the federal government in hopes of landing a military base. Following the refunding of the PWA in that same year, contractors and their workers, along with workers from the WPA and CCC, descended on the area to begin construction of MacDill Army Air Field. In the Panhandle, the federal government moved to purchase 350,000 acres of raw land to create the Choctahatchee Bombing Range, which was used by AAF and navy pilots to practice their bombing skills. Other navy bases, such as the Pensacola Naval Air Station, received PWA funds to upgrade their facilities. When war came in 1941, the PWA morphed into the Federal War Administration, and other agencies dedicated building and maintaining military bases and in producing armaments. By war's end in 1945, the Sunshine State was home to more than ninety military installations of all kinds and had seen more than 2.5 million trainees go through programs at them.

More than any other New Deal program, the PWA epitomized the Rooseveltian notion of "priming the pump" as a means of getting the American economy restarted. Between July 1933 and March 1939, the PWA funded and administered the construction of more than 34,000 projects including airports, large electricity-generating dams, bridges and major

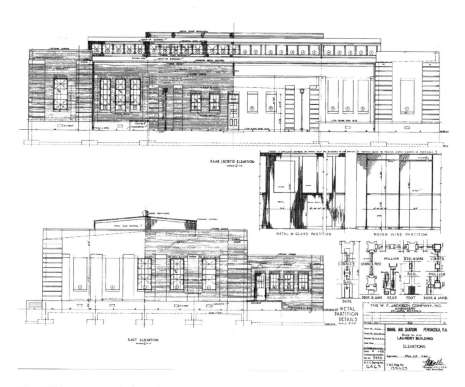

The PWA constructed a large laundry building at the Pensacola Naval Air Station to handle the needs of the large numbers of trainees who came to learn how to operate from the decks of carriers. *Courtesy of the Library of Congress.*

warships for the navy. Seventy percent of all the new schools and one-third of all the hospitals built between 1933 and 1939 were constructed through the PWA. Road projects accounted for most of the PWA projects (some 11,428 were undertaken) and consumed over 15 percent of the agency's budget. Additional projects were created through PWA grants to other New Deal agencies, including the WPA and CCC.

Was the PWA successful? Some economists look at the PWA spending and note that the infusion of money did little to dramatically change the American employment crisis. Unemployment was higher after the creation of the PWA and did not decline until the outbreak of World War II. Other economists note, however, that without the massive expenditure of PWA funds, millions of Americans would have had to be on relief. For those who found work on PWA projects, what mattered most was how the PWA programs changed their lives.

Chapter 17

THE VERY OLD AND THE VERY YOUNG

I hereby prescribe the following functions and duties of the National Youth Administration:
To initiate and administer a program of approved projects which shall provide relief, work relief, and employment for persons between the ages of sixteen and twenty-five years who are no longer in regular attendance at a school requiring full time, and who are not regularly engaged in remunerative employment.
—*Franklin Delano Roosevelt, Executive Order 7086, June 26, 1935*

Security was attained in the earlier days through the interdependence of members of families upon each other and of the families within a small community upon each other. The complexities of great communities and of organized industry make less real these simple means of security. Therefore, we are compelled to employ the active interest of the Nation as a whole through government in order to encourage a greater security for each individual who composes it...This seeking for a greater measure of welfare and happiness does not indicate a change in values. It is rather a return to values lost in the course of our economic development and expansion.
—*Franklin D. Roosevelt, Message of the President to Congress, June 8, 1934*

By 1930, there were two groups of Americans that were desperate for relief but fell outside the WPA programs—the young, who were in high school or college and needed money to stay in school, and the elderly, who could not participate in work programs because of illness, age or a lack of usable skills. The Census of 1930 recorded approximately 12.9 million Americans sixty-five years old and older, or about 5.4 percent of the total population. The same census put the total of young Americans ages fifteen to twenty-four years at 21 million, or 18.3 percent of the population. In the

The Very Old and the Very Young

Sunshine State, the numbers were higher than the national figures. Floridians above the age of sixty numbered 112,387, or 7.7 percent of the population of 1,468,211 identified in the 1930 Census. Young Floridians between the ages of fifteen and twenty-four numbered 276,104, or 18.8 percent of the population.

For New Deal planners, the question of whether to pay special attention to these two groups or to try to incorporate them into the mainstream of relief efforts was an important one. If they ignored either, the labor force, already exceeding the number of available jobs, would become even more crowded as the young and the old entered the job market in order to survive. Wages would be further diminished, and the Depression would deepen. The obvious solution was to develop programs that would keep the young in school and the old at home. There were 111,662 Floridians between the ages of fifteen and eighteen—the prime years for high school—but as conditions worsened, many of these were considering leaving school to support themselves or their families. Many young Americans had left school to find jobs to help with the family household, but there were no jobs to be

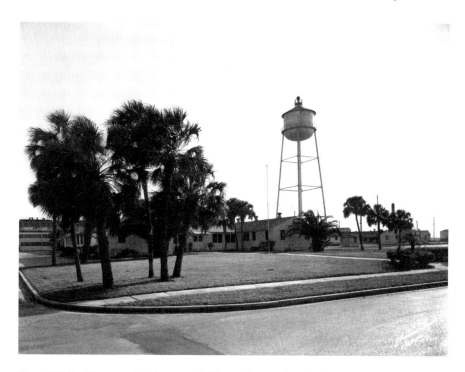

Drew Field in Tampa, which is currently Tampa International Airport, was a PWA project undertaken as part of FDR's war preparation program. *Courtesy of the Anthony Pizzo Collection, University of South Florida.*

had, particularly for unskilled and undereducated young Americans. Youths between sixteen and twenty-five years of age represented about one-third of the unemployed, and nationwide about 2.25 million students dropped out of school looking for jobs. Thus, there was a clear need to "warehouse" these potential workers until jobs became available.

An additional 164,442 youths in Florida were of college age (nineteen to twenty-four), although the number looking to acquire a degree in higher education was very small. In 1930, the entire college student population numbered only around 7,000 in the state, or just 4.3 percent of those in the age group. The remainder was in the state's labor pool, drawing relief or working on CCC and WPA projects. In *Looking for the New Deal*, Elna C. Green's collection of letters from women in Florida during the Depression, there appear two recurring themes—the need for some kind of assistance to keep children in school and some form of old age relief.

On June 26, 1935, FDR took the first step in providing financial assistance to students in high school and college. The National Youth Administration created work programs for Americans between the ages of sixteen and twenty-five. Although the NYA did not cover all those in need, it did eventually provide "work study" jobs for 327,000 high school and college students, paying wages from six to forty dollars a month. Some 155,000 youths from relief families were paid ten to twenty-five dollars a month for part-time work that included janitorial services, repair and minor construction projects, library work and work in school offices.

Administered nationally by Alabamian Aubrey Willis Williams, the NYA had an annual budget of approximately $58 million. Mary McLeod Bethune, the founder of Bethune-Cookman College and a close friend of Eleanor Roosevelt, served as the national director of the Negro Unit of the NYA. Although he was from Alabama, Williams was a New Deal liberal and ensured that whites and blacks had opportunities for funding under the NYA. Unlike other New Deal agencies, the NYA included both males and females as recipients of funds.

Working closely with the WPA, the NYA operated summer camps, many of which included dormitory facilities. In Florida, the NYA operated Camp Roosevelt near Ocala, an encampment that had originally been constructed to house WPA workers on the trans-Florida canal and several other camps in cooperation with the CCC. It was described as "a 154 acre site with 100 buildings including 78 modern houses for staff and students, two dormitories, a dining hall, lecture hall, office buildings and other structures...made available by the federal government for the division to operate an extensive adult education program. In all, ninety-four non-credit courses were offered

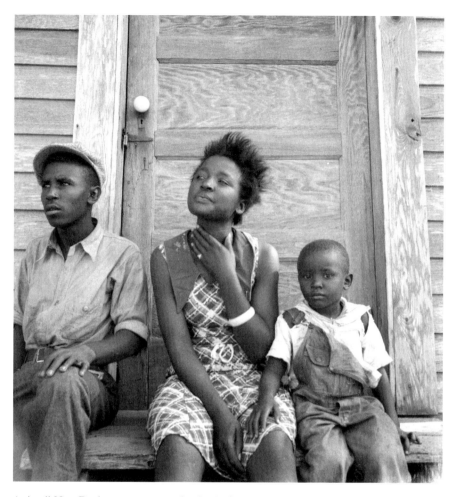

As in all New Deal programs operating in the South, a code of strict segregation was observed. These young African Americans were part of the National Youth Administration program for blacks located in Live Oak. *Courtesy of the Library of Congress.*

at this facility with a total of 4,206 students in attendance." Students were restricted as to the number of hours they could work; usually they were limited to eight hours a day, forty hours a week or a cumulative total of seventy hours a month. Their earnings usually ranged from ten to twenty-five dollars a month, a portion of which was sent home to their families. Unlike other WPA programs, the amounts paid to students did not count as family income or reduce the amount of money available for family relief. A strict policy of segregation was adhered to in the joint NYA and CCC programs, just as it was in other New Deal programs in the South.

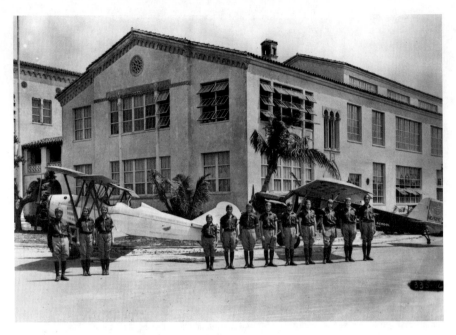

Students enrolled in the NYA learned a variety of skills while earning a small stipend. Pictured here, Coral Cables High School students learn the rudiments of aviation. *Courtesy of Arva Parks McCabe.*

Students enrolled in the NYA were offered the opportunity to take a variety of self-improvement courses, which ranged from citizenship courses and courses in personal hygiene to vocational training, nursing courses and domestic science. Additionally, the NYA created educational camps for unemployed females between the ages of eighteen and twenty-five where occupational skills and interpersonal skills were taught. Some courses elicited complaints from the public, which viewed them as having little economic value and wasteful of public funds. In his 2004 thesis, "The New Deal and Higher Education in Florida, 1933–1939: Temporary Assistance and Tacit Promises," Larry R. Smith noted two such complaints (italics mine):

> *A few of Camp Roosevelt's courses elicited pointed remarks from the public. A Jacksonville lawyer sent a testy letter to Tigert, enclosing a pamphlet advertising "Two Short Courses in Personal Grooming" that were held in January 1937. Programs included: "What is a Well-Dressed Woman; Anatomy of Skin and Hair; Line and Design; Budgeting and Buying." In the lawyer's opinion, the course was "an attempt to make silk purses out of sows' ears and is a fine illustration of modern trends." He pointed out*

that the "circular does not indicate that persons of color are eligible, but I should think that several of the courses would be of particular interest to them.*" Indeed, the pamphlet listed "Comments on the Course by Prominent Citizens" which noted that the courses "are offered to* all women in Florida, regardless of social standing or economic status," *without mentioning race. Another lawyer called the course "such a lot of foolishness (and) a waste of the tax payers' money," and he reproached UF, declaring that it "could use its time and money" for more constructive purposes.*

When J.R.E. Lee (president of the all-black Florida A&M College) wrote to John J. Tigert (University of Florida president) requesting that his students be allowed to participate in programs at Camp Roosevelt, Tigert responded by citing the prohibition against race-mixing in Florida schools in the Florida constitution but promised to help create a similar camp for blacks. African Americans were offered many of the same kinds of courses, although in segregated camps and on the campuses of black colleges. One all-black residential camp operated by the NYA was located near Live Oak. As the national director of the Negro NYA, Mary McLeod Bethune was able to direct funding to her institution in Daytona Beach. Although she was headquartered in Washington, the Bethune-Cookman staff created model programs that emphasized practical and marketable skills. Funding from the NYA also provided financial stability for this private black college, which survived the Depression in reasonable financial shape. Florida A&M College also developed its own programs and enjoyed a great deal of success in its literacy program, which drew students from black enrollees in the CCC.

Public and private white colleges in the Sunshine State also used NYA funding to restore faculty salaries and supplement campus construction funding. University of Florida was under the leadership of John J. Tigert, a progressive leader who had served as the national commissioner of education in the 1920s. When asked by Aubrey Williams to take the reins of the NYA in Florida, he refused and pushed the candidacy of Robert C. Beaty, the assistant dean of student affairs at the university. Beaty was selected, but Tigert retained a great deal of influence on what New Deal programs did in the state, where WPA funds were spent on higher education programs and what amount of funds went where.

The NYA was a resounding success for FDR and the New Deal planners. From the beginning, it was aimed at a specific clientele of young Americans

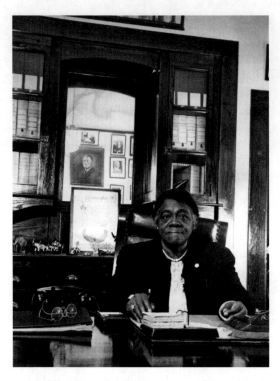

Mary McLeod Bethune, the president of Bethune-Cookman College, served as the national director for the Negro NYA and was influential in bringing federal dollars to all-black colleges in Florida. *Courtesy of the Library of Congress.*

and was administered by professional educators and social workers. None of the allocated funds were expended until the initial program had been approved by two oversight committees created by Roosevelt. The first was the Executive Committee, headed by Assistant Secretary of the Treasury Josephine Roche and other federal officials. The other was the National Advisory Committee, headed by Charles W. Taussig—a Roosevelt intimate, a member of the "Brain Trust" and the president of the American Molasses Company—and consisting of thirty-five representatives from American industry, agriculture, youth and educational institutions. Meeting once annually, the Advisory Committee evaluated NYA policies and programs and made recommendations for future activities. Such deliberate planning and constant review were not hallmarks of many New Deal programs, but this cautious and deliberate approach ensured success for the NYA. Although constantly fighting budget battles with conservatives in Congress and opponents at the state level, the NYA continued to operate until 1943, when the need for it vanished under full wartime employment. Even today, many American adults—black and white—have fond memories of this New Deal program.

The problem of elderly poverty in the United States was a difficult one facing Franklin Delano Roosevelt. To not develop a special plan to provide relief for this segment of the population would mean that the unemployment rolls would continue to increase as people sixty-five and older desperately tried to support themselves by taking jobs, often for lesser wages, that could

The Very Old and the Very Young

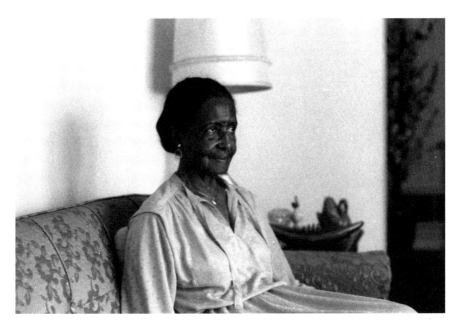

A teacher for more than thirty years in Manatee County, Florine Jones Able was an unusual woman. Married and the mother of a baby, she left Manatee County—and her husband—to pursue a degree at Savannah State College in 1932. *Courtesy of the Manatee Public Library System.*

be filled by younger people. In 1933, Dr. Francis E. Townsend articulated a plan to provide $200 a month to the elderly, paid for from the public treasury. What was initially a rambling "Letter to the Editor" soon became a formal plan that would become the basis for a massive political movement. Townsend's proposal became a rallying cry for the elderly and a serious concern to the political fortunes of FDR. In addition, the radical nature of the proposal, coupled with its popularity, frightened the wealthy class of Americans, who viewed the unemployed masses with suspicion.

In the Sunshine State, the Townsend Plan engendered a great deal of support among the state's elderly population, which had grown during the previous three decades. In St. Petersburg, which was already known as a haven for the elderly, the *St. Petersburg Times* threw its editorial support behind the movement, and that city became a center for "Townsendnites." On December 18, 1934, Mrs. Charles A. Stephens of Miami sent a letter to Eleanor Roosevelt explaining how the Townsend proposal would help: "It would do away with poorhouses which cost tremendously…and I believe as many are claiming that by millions being compelled to spend their $200 monthly [payment] & creating such a

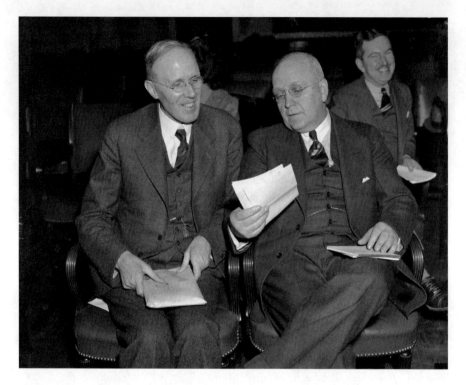

The Townsend Plan, an early plan to provide assistance for the elderly in America, was very popular. The emergence of a strong movement demanding the plan be enacted into federal legislation spurred FDR to create his own plan—Social Security. *Courtesy of the Burgert Brothers Collection, Tampa Public Library.*

stir of buying & circulation of money that it would end the [D]epression very quickly." Stephens's views were echoed by Della Harper of Orlando, who wrote to Eleanor Roosevelt on December 31, 1934: "[The Townsend Plan] will not only make the old people independnet [*sic*] but will inable [*sic*] them to relief so many others that are striving to help themselves and their dependents and cannot through no fault of the own."

Although the Townsend Plan was considered too radical and too costly by some political and economic leaders, it was a modest proposal when compared to the "Share the Wealth" proposal of Senator Huey "Kingfish" Long of Louisiana. A former governor and a nominal Democrat, Long espoused the radical populist rhetoric that was popular in the South and attacked banks, stockbrokers and bankers, as well as individuals who inherited wealth. He considered the Roosevelt administration to be in cahoots with the wealthy and declared himself in opposition to the New Deal because it was too modest in nature. In the Senate, Long introduced measures that called for the confiscation and redistribution of the nation's wealth—measures that were considered so extreme they were never reported out of committee to the full Senate. On February 23, 1934, he stole a page from FDR's playbook and made a nationwide radio address entitled "Every Man a King." Relying on his folksy oratorical style and biblical references while playing on ingrained class prejudices, he outlined his plan for the average American: "[T]hat there should be a guaranty [*sic*] of a family wealth of around $5,000; enough for a home, an automobiles, a radio, and the ordinary conveniences, and the opportunity to educate their children; a fair share of the income of this land…so there will be no such thing as a family living in poverty and distress." For many Americans sixty years old and older, Long proposed a pension of $30 a month but cautioned his listeners that this was not for everyone. "Now, we do not give this pension to a man making $1,000 a year, and we do not give it to him if he has $10,000 in property, but outside of that we do."

For the wealthy class, he promised to "take the billion-dollar fortunes and strip them down to frying size." Under his proposal, private fortunes would be limited to $50 million (possibly as little as $10 million if the need arose for more money to pay for public programs), legacies to $5 million and annual incomes to $1 million. Long's attack on wealth in America and his call for wealth redistribution caused the moneyed class and the social conservative politicians to rail against him. He attracted a great deal of support among the ranks of the nation's poor, despite the fact that FDR called him "one of two of the most dangerous men in America." With his popularity rising, Long considered joining forces with xenophobic Father Charles Coughlin to create a national political party that would carry him into the White House. Whether or not this would have been possible will never be known, because on September 8, 1935, Dr. Carl Weiss, the son-in-law of a Long political rival in Louisiana, shot him. Two days later, Long died. Roosevelt and his supporters breathed a sigh of relief.

Both the Townsend Plan and Long's "Share the Wealth" proposal prompted FDR to come up with a plan of his own to address the needs of the elderly. On June 8, 1934, in a message to Congress, President Roosevelt outlined a plan to create a new system of relief for older Americans. He appointed five cabinet officials to a Committee on Economic Security (CES) and directed them to study the problem of the economic insecurity of the elderly and to make recommendations for legislative programs to provide a modicum of relief for them. After extensive research, the committee delivered its report to FDR, who then forwarded it to Congress with a call for remedial legislation. After prolonged hearings and reconciliation conferences, Congress passed the Social Security Act, which was signed into law by Roosevelt on August 14, 1935.

The law contained two major provisions—a system of grants to fund state welfare programs for the elderly on a temporary basis and the establishment of a program of benefits to be paid to the primary wage earner in a family when he or she retired at age sixty-five. Funding for the retirement benefits was based on payroll tax contributions paid jointly by the worker and the employer over his or her working life. The first payroll taxes would be collected in 1937. Monthly payments were originally scheduled to begin in 1943, but this date was later advanced to 1940. State grant funding began immediately after the law was signed, but additional funding for other parts of the bill was delayed until early 1936.

It took almost a full year for the Social Security Board—the governing unit—to develop rules and regulations and to print and distribute explanatory literature. More than thirty million Social Security numbers were assigned and cards issued during this time, and 151 field offices were established. In January 1937, the first Federal Insurance Contributions Act (FICA) taxes were collected and the first lump-sum payments made. These payments were made to provide instant relief for elderly workers and to take them out of the workforce. The first individual to receive a lump-sum payment was Ernest Ackerman of Cleveland, who retired one day after the collection of taxes began. His check? A total of seventeen cents, but not the lowest amount ever paid through the program, which was five cents! On average, eligible retirees received a single payment of $58.06.

Townsend and his followers were bitterly disappointed with Social Security because it did not deliver monthly payments in 1935 and because the benefits Social Security promised were small compared to the $200 per month that Townsend and his followers wanted. The fact that people had to work under the Social Security program to earn payments provoked additional criticisms. Despite the dissatisfaction of the Townsend crowd, Social Security became a reality and continues in a modified form today.

Chapter 18
STRANGE FRUIT

Southern trees bear a strange fruit,
Blood on the leaves and blood at the root,
Black bodies swinging in the Southern breeze,
Strange fruit hanging from the poplar trees.
—*Poem by Abel Meeropol (1939) and sung by Billie Holiday*

The Planter lives off the sweat of the sharecroppers brow/Just how the
sharecropper lives the planter cares not how.
—*John Handcox, "The Planter and the Sharecropper" (1935)*

If the Latin community was unhappy with the WPA, it was not alone. For many white southerners, the WPA had the overall effect of challenging the status quo of the Jim Crow system of segregation by empowering African Americans and paying them higher wages than were paid in the private labor market. W.M. Rowlett, a Tampa physician, wrote to Claude Pepper on November 2, 1938, complaining that black women working in sewing rooms made more than a black woman working as a maid for his daughter. "How long," he asked, "will the solid south remain solid when the negro [*sic*] is permitted to insult our white citizens believing that they have the backing of our government?" This was a constant refrain from white southerners who opposed African Americans receiving any relief money or employment from the federal government. Lorena Hickock, who had undertaken a survey of the country for Harry Hopkins in 1933, reported the same attitude prevailed throughout the South. David M. Kennedy wrote in *Freedom from Fear: The American People in Depression and War, 1929–1945* that Hickock was appalled when a relief director in Savannah told her, "Any Nigger who gets over $8 a week is a spoiled Nigger, that's all…The Negroes…regard the President as the Messiah, and they think that…they'll all be getting $12 a week for the rest of their lives."

Faced with a declining black labor force in the years between 1910 and 1930, white landowners were concerned that federal relief programs would further shrink the pool of available workers and therefore erode their wealth. The migration of African Americans from the old southern agricultural belt slowed to a trickle during the Depression because northern industries had no need for more workers—they could not find jobs for all of the whites who wanted to work. Peonage, sharecropping and tenancy—labor forms that tended to hold blacks in place in the labor market—were weakened, but as Jay R. Mandle wrote in his *Roots of Black Poverty*, they remained in place throughout the 1930s. Any large-scale relief program by the federal government would almost certainly destroy them.

In Florida, peonage, sharecropping and tenancy persisted in the northern part of the state (which had constituted the antebellum plantation belt), in the citrus-producing areas of middle and southern Florida and in the turpentine and lumber industries in the northern and central parts of the state. Lorena Hickock, Hopkins's eyes and ears, castigated Florida citrus growers who had "the world licked…for being mean-spirited, selfish, and irresponsible." Her anger grew as she visited state after state in the South: "The truth is that the rural South never has progressed beyond slave labor." She further fumed, "When their slaves were taken away they proceeded to establish a system of peonage that was as close to slavery as it possibly could be and included Whites as well as Blacks."

For decades, the large farmers beat back effort after effort to destroy the oppressive forms of labor, and with the advent of the New Deal relief programs, they mobilized their allies to curtail the extension of relief to their workers. With a mandate that called for the awarding of relief without regard to race, the CWA, and later the WPA, disrupted the established system of Jim Crow, forcing the wage levels in the South to gradually rise. Farmers and growers fought back by ensuring that individuals sympathetic to their efforts were appointed to local relief boards, which had the initial responsibility for certifying individuals for WPA work and for awarding eligibility for relief. When relief awards moved from local board selections to means tests administered by hired social workers, large farmers turned to other methods of control.

Strange Fruit

In the South, the ultimate method of control was to resort to lynching. Florida had a long history of lynching both African Americans and whites who were considered threats to the established social and economic system. Walter T. Howard focused his attention on the Sunshine State in his book, *Lynchings: Extralegal Violence in Florida During the 1930s*, and detailed twelve lynchings of blacks during the decade, all of which followed a pattern that had been established the decade before. Immediately after the end of World War I, white southerners used lynchings to reestablish white dominance in the region—a dominance they felt had been sorely tested by African American soldiers returning from France. From 1917 to 1927, 444 black men were lynched across the nation, and Florida accounted for 47 of these deaths. Florida was also the setting for the infamous Rosewood massacre in 1923, where in the course of four days the entire town was burned and several blacks killed. Howard points out that using violence as a way to rigidly enforce the Jim Crow system "paid off in numerous ways, including…providing a large pool of black workers who were easily exploited and manipulated."

Even after the passage of the Agricultural Adjustment Act of 1932, which paid famers to reduce their acreage of crops and therefore reduce the need for labor, southerners were uncomfortable with the idea that African Americans would no longer be wholly dependent on them for employment. The federal government's policy of paying landowners the subsidies for taking land out of production ignored the claims of tenant farmers and sharecroppers that they too were entitled to a share of the subsidies. Most of these tenants and sharecroppers were simply let go—without any source of replacement income and without any source of sustenance. It was a case of the federal government attempting to help southern agriculture without taking into consideration the unique labor arrangements. David Conrad's 1965 book, *The Forgotten Farmers: The Story of Sharecroppers in the New Deal*, examined the problems and concluded that white landowners evicted their tenants because "if [they] evicted tenants [they] would not have to support them, [they] would not have to split government benefit money with them, and [they] would use the rented acres for [their] own purposes."

In 1933, Roosevelt created the $500 million Federal Emergency Relief Administration to help poor rural Americans. Local selection boards determined the recipients of FERA aid, and although black farmers applied for relief, they did not receive it as often as whites. The average monthly total of relief checks for whites was $19.51—for blacks it was $15.17. The disparity in relief payments reflected not only preferential treatment for whites but also the racist belief that African Americans could survive on less.

Those blacks who complained about differences in relief payments risked being labeled "uppity" and were subjected to violence.

The African American community had hope that something might change to alter black-white relations in the South, and they pinned their hopes on Roosevelt. After FDR's election in 1932, Walter White and the National Association for the Advancement of Colored People pressed him to sponsor an anti-lynching law in Congress. Roosevelt, who had condemned lynch law as "collective murder" in a December 6, 1933 radio address, was reluctant to do so because he feared the loss of the votes of southern politicians whose support he needed to enact and preserve his New Deal programs against Republican attacks. A new generation of Americans, he said, "seeks action…and is not content with preaching against that vile form of collective murder—lynch law—which has broken out in our midst anew." However, even after Eleanor Roosevelt, at the urging of White and Mary McLeod Bethune, pressed FDR to support a bill against lynching, he refused to do so.

Florida was the scene of two gruesome lynchings in 1934 and 1935. The first, which happened in Marianna, supposedly happened because the victim, Claude Neal, murdered his white lover, Lola Cannidy. Witnesses later said that Cannidy actually had a white lover and that Neal was merely a neighbor. Neal was arrested and transported to Alabama to ensure his safety. Florida newspapers announced that Neal would be lynched in Marianna, and a crowd of somewhere between three thousand and seven thousand gathered there. On October 26, 1934, he was taken from the jail and brought to Marianna to face the mob. What followed was a scene of unspeakable horror. As one witness recalled:

> *After taking the nigger to the woods about four miles from Greenwood, they cut off his penis. He was made to eat it. Then they cut off his testicles and made him eat them and say he liked it. Then they sliced his sides and stomach with knives and every now and then somebody would cut off a finger or toe. Red hot irons were used on the nigger to burn him from top to bottom. From time to time during the torture a rope would be tied around Neal's neck and he was pulled up over a limb and held there until he almost choked to death when he would be let down and the torture begin all over again. After several hours of this unspeakable torture, they decided just to kill him.*

Once he was dead, Neal's body was tied to a rope attached to the rear bumper of an automobile and dragged over the highway to the home of Lola Cannidy. Once there, the body was further mutilated by onlookers.

His body was then taken back to Marianna and hanged on a tree on the courthouse square. Pictures were taken of the mutilated body and sold for fifty cents each. Neal's fingers and toes were sold as souvenirs to the crowd that arrived too late to witness the gory festivities.

Newspapers around the nation were quick to feature the Neal lynching on their front pages. Waves of condemnation followed quickly, and the anti-lynching movement gained momentum. Scarcely had the outrage at the Neal lynching calmed down when another Florida lynching took over the front pages. Rubin Stacy, a homeless tenant farmer, had approached the home of Marion Jones in Fort Lauderdale to beg for food. Jones, who was frightened by the man's appearance, screamed for help. Stacy was arrested on July 19, and six deputies were assigned to escort him to jail in Miami. A mob of around one hundred masked men stopped the car and seized the black man. Robert Nolin reported what happened next in the July 17, 2010 issue of the *Sun Sentinel*:

> *On the morning of July 19, Stacey* [sic] *was arrested after Jones identified him as her assailant. "He bears several knife scars testifying to previous bad character and bore the nickname among his people of 'Gruff,'" the* Fort Lauderdale Daily News *reported.*
>
> *Late that afternoon, Sheriff Walter Clark and his brother, Chief Deputy Bob Clark, decided to move Stacey to a Miami jail for "safekeeping."*
>
> *Six deputies escorting Stacey said they were overpowered by 100 masked men who ran their car off the road and grabbed the suspect. They drove Stacey to a wooded area near Jones' home, snatched the clothesline that had snagged him earlier and hanged him from a scrub pine. He was handcuffed, clad in overalls and a long-sleeve white shirt.*
>
> *"They just picked him up with the rope from the ground, didn't bother to push him from an automobile or anything," Deputy Virgil Wright, one of the escorts, told the newspaper.*
>
> *An unidentified woman who was a teenager at the time told the* Sun Sentinel *in 1994 that she participated in the lynching. It was Deputy Bob Clark, she said, who tossed the line over a branch and slowly raised Stacey off the ground.*
>
> *He then told the 25 to 30 people gathered there that they had to take part, the woman said. He passed his pistol around. People took turns firing into Stacey's swaying body, the woman said.*

Once again, Florida dominated the nation's news—but it was not alone. During the 1930s, forty-six lynchings took place throughout the nation. There were fifteen lynchings of blacks in 1934 and twenty-one in 1935, but that number fell to eight in 1936, three in 1937 and two in 1939. Some conservatives, such as William E. Borah of Idaho, took comfort in the fact that the number of mob actions tapered off by the end of the decade and vigorously opposed any attempt to pass a federal law criminalizing lynching. There had been more than two hundred separate anti-lynching laws introduced in Congress since 1908, but while some of these managed to get passed in the House of Representatives, southern opposition in the Senate always managed to stop their final passage.

In 1935, Robert F. Wagner, a senator from New York, and Edward P. Costigan, a senator from Colorado, agreed to co-sponsor an anti-lynching bill. Like the ill-fated Dyer Bill, sponsored by Representative Leonidas C. Dyer of Missouri in 1918, the legislation proposed federal trials, stiff fines and imprisonment for any law enforcement officers who failed to exercise their responsibilities during a lynching incident. Wagner, who had been friends with FDR since they were youths in New York and was a staunch New Deal supporter, tried to persuade him to support the proposed bill. Roosevelt refused because he was up for reelection and wanted to curry favor with Democrats in the South.

When the Costigan-Wagner Bill was brought before the Senate in January 1938, Old South Democrats launched a filibuster, which lasted more than two weeks. Newly elected Charles O. Andrews and the up-for-reelection Claude Pepper were leaders in the effort to defeat the bill. Pepper, who was a supporter of most New Deal programs, sided with the conservatives and spoke for eleven hours one day alone. Andrews also shouldered a similar burden in the Senate debate, while in Florida, the most recent former governor, David Sholtz, was joined by another former governor, Doyle E. Carlton, and newly inaugurated governor Fred P. Cone in denouncing the bill. Pepper argued that many southerners were already working to end lynching and asked, "Are their efforts to be stigmatized by such humiliating coercion as is attempted by the proposed legislation?"

Faced with a unified effort of senators from southern states and lacking the support of Roosevelt, the Costigan-Wagner Bill went down to defeat. Pepper reminded the *Pensacola Daily News* during his reelection campaign in 1938 that he had been instrumental in the defeat and that he would continue to do everything in his power against any attempt to pass another such bill. Despite the high hopes of the African American

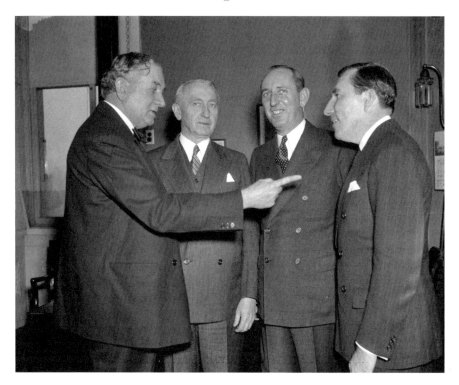

Senators Tom Connally (D-Texas), Walter F. George (D-Georgia), Richard Russell (D-Georgia) and Claude Pepper (D-Florida) plan their strategy to defeat the anti-lynching bill in the United States Senate. They managed to do so after a filibuster that lasted twenty days. *Courtesy of the Library of Congress.*

community, FDR refused to throw his influence behind the anti-lynching bill. Attempts by the Justice Department to prosecute lynchers under Reconstruction-era civil rights statutes met with failure. It was not until 1946 that a conviction for lynching was ever attained.

Roosevelt's concern about keeping the votes of Democrats in the South was more of a smokescreen than anything else. The New Deal was extremely popular with the electorate and the South in particular, and in 1936, Roosevelt had easily defeated the Republican Party candidate, Alfred M. Landon, by 27,751,612 votes to 16,681,913 in the popular vote and 523 to 8 in the Electoral College. In 1940, he trounced Republican Wendell Willkie, carrying all the southern states by margins well above 50 percent. In the Electoral College, he received 449 votes to Willkie's 82.

In July 1935, Robert C. Weaver, the adviser on Negro affairs in the Department of the Interior, wrote an article for *Opportunity: A Journal of*

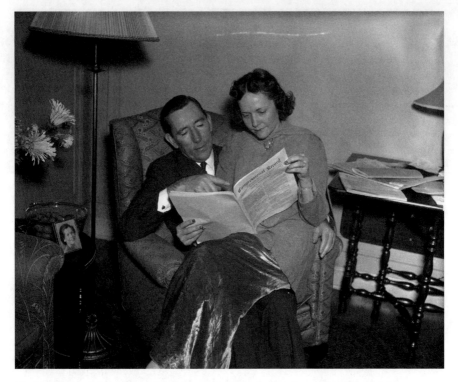

Florida Senator Claude Pepper points out the "good" press he received due to his participation in the filibuster against the anti-lynching bill. He spoke one day for eleven hours straight. *Courtesy of the Library of Congress.*

Negro Life entitled "The New Deal and the Negro: A Look at the Facts." His take on the impact of the New Deal on the African American community was laudatory:

> *In the execution of some phases of the Recovery Program, there have been difficulties, and the maximum results have not been received by the Negroes. But, given the economic situation of 1932, the New Deal has been more helpful than harmful to Negroes. We had unemployment in 1932. Jobs were being lost by Negroes, and they were in need. Many would have starved had there been no Federal relief program. As undesirable as is the large relief load among Negroes, the FERA has meant much to them. In most of the New Deal setups, there has been some Negro representation by competent Negroes. The Department of the Interior and the PWA have appointed some fifteen Negroes to jobs of responsibility which pay good salaries. These persons have secretarial and clerical staffs attached to*

their offices. In addition to these new jobs, there are the colored messengers, who number around 100 and the elevator operators for the Government buildings, of whom there are several hundred. This is not, of course, adequate representation; but it represents a step in the desired direction and is greater recognition than has been given Negroes in the Federal Government during the last 20 years.

Although Weaver might have been upbeat about the achievements of the New Deal, the simple fact was that racism permeated all of the federal agencies. As late as 1941, Edgar Brown of the CCC authored a pamphlet entitled "The CCC and Colored Youth," which listed the number of blacks enrolled in the agency and their accomplishments. Although the pamphlet was aimed at demonstrating how involved America's African American community was in this particular program, Brown referred to "colored youth" and "colored boys" throughout the brochure and used the word "Negro" only twice in a total of 1,642 words. One suspects that the same is true of brochures printed by other New Deal agencies.

Although the actual accomplishments of the Roosevelt administration in ending racism and racial violence were minimal, the fact that African Americans were even included in New Deal programs counted with the black community. By the end of the New Deal, the majority of African Americans had abandoned their allegiance to the Republicans, the party of Lincoln, and become Democrats—and that remains the case today.

Chapter 19

PREPARING FOR THE WAR AND ENDING THE DEPRESSION

The test of our progress is not whether we add more to the abundance of those who have too much: it is whether we provide enough for those who have too little…I see one-third of a nation ill-housed, ill-clothed, ill nourished.
—*Franklin Delano Roosevelt, Second Inaugural Address, 1937*

Every realist knows that the democratic way of life is at this moment being directly assailed in every part of the world—assailed either by arms, or by secret spreading of poisonous propaganda by those who seek to destroy unity and promote discord in nations that are still at peace.
—*Franklin Delano Roosevelt, Annual Message to the Congress, January 6, 1941*

Despite the best efforts of the Roosevelt administration to end massive unemployment, the Depression continued full bore in 1937, 1938 and 1939. Florida was better off than many of the more industrialized states, but it still suffered. Although tourism was making a strong comeback and the state's citrus and cattle industries had recovered to pre-Depression levels, the movement of rural populations into cities and towns made a full recovery difficult. Without a doubt, the Sunshine State had profited from the make-work programs like the WPA, the PWA, the CCC and other New Deal programs. Three model farm communities had been created by the Farm Resettlement Administration, and more than one hundred airports had been built or improved. Small communities and large cities saw the construction of municipal buildings, post offices, low-cost housing projects, hospitals and improved infrastructure systems. Colleges and universities profited as well, witnessing WPA and PWA construction projects that offered new amenities to their students. Actors, writers, farmers, men, women, young persons, blacks, whites, Hispanics and countless other Floridians found employment through the various programs of the WPA, while the elderly received relief payments and, ultimately, Social Security checks. Through it all, however, there was a persistent feeling of impermanence—a sense that all of the largesse of the federal programs could end at any time without the economy having made substantial progress. On tenterhooks, Florida's population could take little solace from what was happening on the national scene.

Nationwide, yearly statistics pointed to a recession that was dragging the economy rapidly down to the levels of 1933 and 1934. Industrial production had slumped to about the same level as 1934, while steel production, always a bellwether indicator in an industrialized society, was only at 20 percent of capacity. Joblessness, which had been momentarily stopped by the New Deal relief projects, soared to around 20 percent of the workforce, or eleven million persons. New Deal planners, who had seen so much accomplished during the first five years of Roosevelt's administrations, worried that all the gains would be lost and called for a new round of spending.

Some Americans, impressed with the achievements of a vibrant German economy and a resurgent Italian nation, demanded a more active government, which just might take the form of a fascist state. They demanded more. FDR, just inaugurated for his second term, faced a growing coalition of anti–New Deal forces in Congress composed of old-line Republicans and conservative southern Democrats, who viewed the New Deal as "too much change, too fast." Southern political leaders were especially concerned about the social changes that the New Deal had wrought, while Republicans, who had strong supporters in the business community, saw the New Deal as a direct attack on the basic principles of American capitalism.

Roosevelt, who was becoming more and more involved in events in Asia and Europe, disagreed with his advisors at first but eventually saw a way to stimulate the economy while preparing for the inevitable war that he thought would surely come. He had started the process of preparation quietly and slowly. In 1936, he had issued an executive order that prohibited the use of steel and iron in PWA and WPA construction projects if a substitute material like wood could be used instead. The metal would be saved for use in shipbuilding. PWA and WPA projects were also directed away from public buildings and parks and shifted toward airports and military construction. While these measures provided some cushion of preparedness, they did not

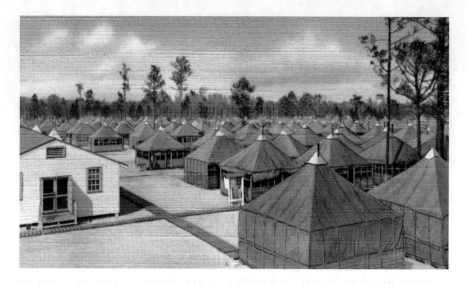

With the passage of the Selective Service and Training Act of 1939, the United States began to aggressively prepare for a war that most Americans were sure would soon involve the United States. Draftees at Camp Blanding lived in "hutments" (canvas shelters) during their training. *Courtesy of the Wynne Collection.*

provide the stimulus that would dramatically revitalize the economy, nor did they provide the essential military tools that would allow for a quick response to any aggression by hostile nations.

The solution to the twin problems of economic recovery and military preparedness seemed very simple—enacting the first ever peacetime draft. A draft would immediately take men out of the labor pool, which was burdened by large numbers of unemployed, and the need for new training facilities and equipment would spur the lagging economy forward. There were two potential roadblocks for Roosevelt, however, and these had to be dealt with before a draft would be approved by Congress. The first problem FDR faced was smoothing the ruffled feathers of his opponents, who were still upset by his ill-fated attempt to increase the number of justices on the Supreme Court in 1937 from nine members to fifteen. Although Roosevelt argued that the sitting justices were elderly, overworked and out of touch with the realities of the New Deal (the Supreme Court had declared several critical pieces of legislation unconstitutional), Congress objected, viewing this proposed expansion as an attempt to expand the power of the presidency. The passage of the Supreme Court Retirement Act on March 1, 1937, was a compromise. It allowed Supreme Court justices to retire at age seventy with full benefits, and one by one the conservative opponents of the New Deal took advantage of the act to retire. Roosevelt swiftly replaced them with men who were amenable to the New Deal—this solution kept the number of justices at nine. The compromise, however, did little to allay the suspicions of anti-FDR opponents in Congress.

The second major problem Roosevelt faced in preparing the United States for the eventuality of war was the persistent isolationist movement, a holdover from the American experience in World War I. Supposedly safe behind the walls of Fortress America—the Atlantic and Pacific Oceans—isolationists argued that any involvement in world affairs would slowly but surely drag the United States into another catastrophic world war. In 1931, President Hoover and Secretary of State Henry L. Stimson had issued the so-called Stimson Doctrine, which stated that the United States would not recognize any territory gained through aggression—this in response to the Japanese invasion of Manchuria. It was a weak condemnation of militarism, and while it placated the "American Firsters" in Congress, it did little to engender respect from aggressor nations.

During Roosevelt's first two terms, world events went through rapid and ominous changes. Italy invaded Ethiopia, Germany reoccupied the Rhineland and annexed Austria and Japan launched an invasion of China. Even the sinking of the American gunboat *Panay* failed to provoke a military response from the United States. The subsequent German invasion of Poland in September 1939 and the declarations of war by France and Great Britain failed to shake Americans out of their comfort zone. Even when Germany, Italy and Japan entered into a formal tri-partite alliance, citizens of the United States remained convinced that they could avoid involvement. The enactment of the Neutrality Acts in 1935 and 1937, which imposed a general embargo on trading in arms and war materials with all parties in a war and declared that American citizens traveling on ships of warring nations traveled at their own risk, added to their sense of complacency.

There were those in the Roosevelt administration, however, who knew the ability of the United States to escape becoming a participant in a world war was wishful thinking. Roosevelt was convinced that it was only a matter of time before some event would trigger American involvement. His personal conviction that war was inevitable led him to reject tradition and stand for an unprecedented third term as president. Even with the certainty he felt about American involvement in a war in the near future, he was compelled to repeatedly assure voters, "I have said this before, but I shall say it again and again—Your boys are not going to be sent into any foreign wars." Although he made this statement on October 30, 1940, Roosevelt had signed the

Selective Training and Service Act of 1940 into law just six weeks earlier on September 16, 1940. The first peacetime conscription in United States history was now the law of the land. The act required men between the ages of twenty-one and thirty-five to register with local draft boards. Later, when the United States entered World War II, all men ages eighteen to forty-five were made subject to military service, and all men ages eighteen to sixty-five were required to register. His election, with only the barest Republican opposition, was assured—the product of the trust and hope he had created with his New Deal policies. The same New Deal agencies that had provided relief work were now oriented toward war preparedness.

In his memoir, *Cornbread, Fatback, and Syrup*, Warren Weekes of Milton left his impression of the times: "Franklin Delano Roosevelt was trying in every way he knew how, politically, to get the United States into a fighting war against Germany. He started in the late 1930s right on until it finally popped the valve in 1941. The CCC was a way that helped prepare our country for war." The army had played an important role in organizing and supervising the CCC, cooking, marching and housing the men in barracks just as if they were in boot camp. Warren describes his days in the corps: "It means they took young volunteers, men, seventeen to twenty-five years old, and they put them in a barracks. They planted trees, fought fires, dug irrigation ditches, and things like that. They had to march with their shovel, or their ax or whatever they were toting that day. They had to follow orders. They had to eat in a building that was for them, the Mess Hall. The meals were prepared by Army cooks." No one complained either. It was thirty dollars a month, of which twenty-five was sent home to support the family, and a young man with clothing provided, three square meals a day and a roof overhead did not need more than five dollars a month to survive. As Weekes saw it, when the war broke out on that fateful December 7, 1941, "Mr. Roosevelt immediately picked up all the CCC boys and put them in the service. They didn't have to be trained. They had been marching. They knew how to drill. They knew how to eat. They knew how to sleep. The only thing was they gave them a rifle instead of a shovel. You had a well-trained soldier who was 'in the Army now.'"

The need to house and train the 1 million men who were to be called up in the first draft meant that millions of dollars were poured into existing New Deal agencies to build new training centers. Some 800,000 other draftees were to be inducted in state guards and ROTC programs. Although the initial length of service was only twelve months, many seasoned military and diplomatic leaders knew that this short period of service would most likely be extended for the "duration" if war came. Additional millions of dollars were let in contracts to provide the equipment, foodstuffs and uniforms that were also needed. Factories, many of which had been idled through most of the 1930s, were reopened, new workers were hired and assembly lines were restarted. Although America was not at war, the foundation for military success was being built. War was not long in coming.

When France capitulated in June 1940, Japan moved into northern French Indochina. And though the United States had no interest there, Roosevelt imposed an embargo on the sale of steel and scrap metal to the Japanese. After Hitler invaded Russia in June 1941, Japan moved into southern Indochina, and FDR ordered all Japanese financial assets in the United States frozen. While steel and iron were critical to the success of the Japanese military, FDR was reluctant to cut off sales of American oil to Japan because he feared it would cause that nation to invade the Dutch East Indies. Dean Acheson, a state department lawyer, drew up the sanctions in such a way that the Japanese were blocked from purchasing American oil, a move that was not authorized by Roosevelt but one that forced his hand after it was announced. War with Japan was now just a matter of time.

The Sunshine State, which was considered a primary training area for American forces because of its balmy weather, clear skies and diverse terrain, was the beneficiary of many of the war preparation dollars. Throughout the state, federal land agents, often using a variety of guises, began to purchase or lease huge tracts of land for military use. Lands that had been acquired by the Federal Resettlement Administration were turned over to the military, while the many small airports that had been built or upgraded by the PWA and WPA received funds for additional upgrades. Construction workers were hired, and current CCC and WPA enrollees were transferred for labor in building barracks, mess halls, auditoriums, administrative buildings, chapels, theaters and countless smaller buildings, as well as training courses, to transform raw land into viable military posts. By early 1941, the first of the draftees were in camp, many of them faced with the tasks of building their own housing.

In the early months of 1942, the war arrived in the western hemisphere. German U-boats, or submarines, operated freely along the eastern coast of the United States, secure in the knowledge that no American effort would be made to curtail their hunting of merchant vessels carrying essential cargoes for the United Kingdom. After several attacks by German submarines on American ships, FDR announced on September 11, 1941, that he had ordered the navy to assume a more aggressive policy and to sink any

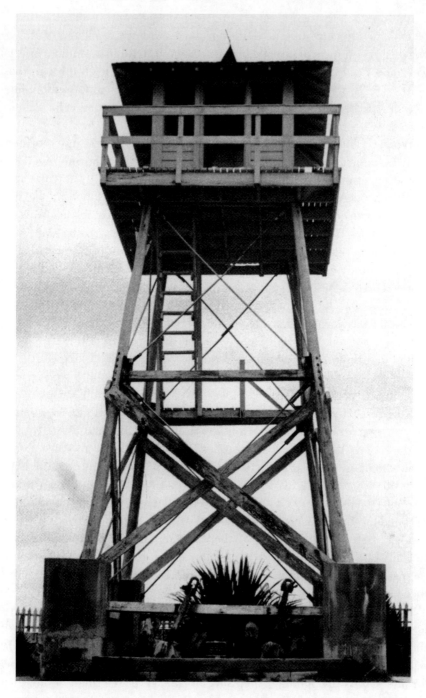

WPA and PWA workers were used to build a string of submarine observation towers along the Florida coasts. Volunteer observers spent long hours keeping watch for enemy activity. *Courtesy of the Wynne Collection.*

Preparing for the War and Ending the Depression

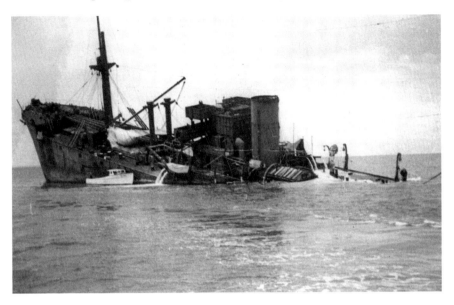

Within days of the Japanese attack on Pearl Harbor and the subsequent declaration of war on the United States by Germany and Italy, German submarines began to sink freighters and tankers off the Florida coast. This is *La Paz*, torpedoed off the shore of Cocoa Beach in early 1942. *Courtesy of the Wynne Collection.*

German or Italian warships found in "waters which we deem necessary for our defense." After the American destroyer *Rueben James* was sunk by U-boats on October 31, 1941, the Neutrality Acts were revised to allow American merchant ships to be armed and to carry American cargoes to nations fighting the Axis powers in Europe. As relations with the Axis powers deteriorated, Roosevelt was more and more certain that war could not be avoided. On December 7, 1941, Japan's sneak attack on the American naval base at Pearl Harbor ended the suspense. America was at war.

As war came in 1941, Florida's recovery from the Depression was assured. Unemployment, which had been above 20 percent in 1935, began to slowly fall with each new military project that was started, eventually reaching an unprecedented 1.5 percent by 1943. Jobs, which had been so scarce in the mid-1930s, became so plentiful that laborers were recruited from as far away as Iowa and Nebraska to fill them. Women and African Americans, long denied meaningful jobs in Florida, were suddenly in demand, as war industries hurried to fill government contracts. Never again would the economy of the Sunshine State be as vibrant. The Great Depression was over.

SELECTED BIBLIOGRAPHY

The literature about the Sunshine State during the 1930s is vast but scattered in a variety of places and formats. Careful searches of the many archives of the historical libraries of the state produce diverse results ranging from personal histories and local photographs to government documents long hidden and forgotten. The key to discovering these sources is to talk with archivists and local historians who know these archives and are more than willing to share them with the serious researcher. Florida is also fortunate to have an enthusiastic group of professional and well-informed amateur historians—these individuals possess a tremendous reserve of knowledge and help to shed light on every aspect of the history of the Sunshine State. To them, we are grateful.

What follows is a selected group of works that cover the highlights of the 1930s. This list is by no means exhaustive, but it will give an indication of the scope of information that is available.

Akerman, Joe A., Jr. *Florida Cowman: A History of Florida Cattle Raising*. Kissimmee: Florida Cattlemen's Association, 1976.

Anderson, James D. *The Education of Blacks in the South, 1860–1935*. Chapel Hill: University of North Carolina Press, 1988.

Boulard, Garry. "'State of Emergency': Key West in the Great Depression." *Florida Historical Quarterly* 67, no. 2 (October 1988): 166–83.

Bray, Sybil Browne. *Marion County Remembers: Salty Crackers*. Ocala, FL: 1984–2003.

Collins, Toni C. "The Civilian Conservation Corps: Putting the Nation to Work." Personal communication. August 28, 2012.

Conrad, David. *The Forgotten Farmers: The Story of Sharecroppers in the New Deal.* Urbana: University of Illinois Press, 1965.

Cox, Merlin G. "David Sholtz: New Deal Governor of Florida." *Florida Historical Quarterly* 43, no. 2 (October 1964): 142–52.

Craton, Michael, and Gail Saunders-Smith. *Islanders in the Stream: A History of the Bahamian People from Aboriginal Times to the End of Slavery.* Athens: University of Georgia Press, 1998.

Dunn, James William. "The New Deal and Florida Politics." PhD diss., University of Florida, 1971.

Farrar, Cecil W., and Margoann Farrar. *Incomparable Delray Beach: Its Early Life and Lore.* Boynton Beach, FL: Star Publishing, Inc., 1974.

Fishback, Price V., and Shawn E. Kantor. "The Adoption of Worker's Compensation in the United States, 1900–1930." *Journal of Law and Economics* 41 (October 1998): 205–341.

Fishback, Price V., William C. Horrace and Shawn Kantor. "The Impact of New Deal Expenditures On Mobility During the Great Depression." *Explorations in Economic History* 43 (2006): 179–222.

Frazer, William, and John J. Guthrie Jr. *The Florida Land Boom: Speculation, Money and the Banks.* Westport, CT: Quorum Books, 1995.

Green, Elna C., ed. *Looking for the New Deal: Florida Women's Letters during the Great Depression.* Columbia: University of South Carolina Press, 2007.

Hopkins, Harry L. *Spending to Save.* New York: W.W. Norton & Company, Inc., 1936.

Howard, Walter T. *Lynchings: Extralegal Violence in Florida during the 1930s.* Selinsgrove, PA: Susquehanna University Press, 1995.

Jarvis, Eric. "'Secrecy Has No Excuse': The Florida Land Boom, Tourism, and the 1926 Smallpox Epidemic in Tampa and Miami." *Florida Historical Quarterly* 89, no. 3 (Winter 2011): 320–46.

Kennedy, David M. *Freedom from Fear: The American People in Depression and War.* New York: Oxford University Press, 1999.

Kennedy, Stetson. *Palmetto Country.* Tallahassee: Florida A&M University Press, 1989.

Kerstein, Robert. *Politics and Growth in Twentieth-Century Tampa.* Gainesville: University Press of Florida, 2001.

Kleinberg, Eliot. *Black Cloud: The Great Florida Hurricane of 1928.* New York: Carroll & Graf Publishers, 2003.

Knowles, Thomas. *Category Five: The 1935 Hurricane in the Florida Keys.* Gainesville: University Press of Florida, 2009.

Lash, Joseph P. *Eleanor and Franklin: The Story of Their Relationship Based on Eleanor Roosevelt's Private Papers.* New York: W.W. Norton & Company, Inc., 1971.

Lempel, Leonard R. "The Mayor's 'Henchmen and Henchwomen, Both

White and Colored': Edward H. Armstrong and the Politics of Race in Daytona Beach, 1900–1940." *Florida Historical Quarterly* 79, no. 3 (Winter 2001): 267–96.

Mandle, Jay R. *The Roots of Black Poverty: The Southern Plantation Economy After the Civil War*. Durham, NC: Duke University Press, 1978.

Margo, Robert. "Employment and Unemployment in the 1930s." *The Cliometric Society*. http://cliometrics.org/conferences/ASSA/Jan_93/Margo%20Abstract/index.html.

McDonogh, Gary W. *The Florida Negro: A Federal Writers' Project Legacy*. Oxford: University of Mississippi Press, 1993.

Melton, Faye Perry. *Memories of Fort McCoy*. Ocala, FL: Typeworld Printing, 1987.

Mishkin, Frederick S. "The Household Balance Sheet and the Great Depression." *Journal of Economic History* 38, no. 4 (December 1978): 918–37.

Mormino, Gary R. *Land of Sunshine, State of Dreams: A Social History of Modern Florida*. Gainesville: University Press of Florida, 2005.

Morris, Allen. *The Florida Handbook, 1991–1992: Florida's People and Their Government*. Tallahassee, FL: Peninsular Publications, 1991.

Morris, Richard B. *Encyclopedia of American History*. New York: Harper & Row, 1961.

Nash, Gerald D. "Herbert Hoover and the Origins of the Reconstruction Finance Corporation." *The Mississippi Valley Historical Review* 46, no. 3 (December 1959): 455–68.

Nelson, David. "Improving Paradise: The Civilian Conservation Corps and Environmental Change in Florida." In *Paradise Lost: The Environmental History of Florida*, edited by Jack E. Davis and Raymond Arsenault. Gainesville: University Press of Florida, 2005.

———. "A New Deal for Welfare: Governor Fred Cone and the Florida State Welfare Board." *Florida Historical Quarterly* 84, no. 2 (Fall 2005): 185–204.

Ortiz, Paul. *Emancipation Betrayed: The Hidden History of Black Organizing and White Violence in Florida from Reconstruction to the Bloody Election of 1920*. Berkeley: University of California Press, 2006.

Rogers, William Warren. "The Great Depression." In *The New History of Florida*, edited by Michael Gannon. Gainesville: University Press of Florida, 1996.

Schlesinger, Arthur M., Jr. *The Coming of the New Deal*. Boston: Houghton Mifflin Company, 1959.

———. *The Crisis of the Old Order, 1919–1933*. Boston: Houghton Mifflin Company, 1957.

Smith, Larry Russell. "The New Deal and Higher Education in Florida,

1933–1939: Temporary Assistance and Tacit Promises." Master's thesis, University of Florida, 2004.

Stockbridge, Frank Parker, and John Holliday Perry. *Florida in the Making.* New York: The de Bower Publishing Co., 1926.

Stronge, William B. *The Sunshine Economy: An Economic History of Florida Since the Civil War.* Gainesville: University Press of Florida, 2008.

Tebeau, Charlton W. *A History of Florida.* Coral Gables, FL: University of Miami Press, 1980.

Tegeder, Michael David. "Economic Boom or Political Boondoggle? Florida's Atlantic Gulf Ship Canal in the 1930s." *Florida Historical Quarterly* 83, no. 1 (Summer 2004): 24–45.

Terkel, Studs. *Hard Times: An Oral History of the Great Depression.* New York: Pantheon Books, 1970.

Tomlinson, Angela E. "Writing Race: The Florida Federal Writer's Project and Racial Identity, 1935–1943." Master's thesis, Florida State University, 2008.

Tucker, Gilbert A. *Before the Timber Was Cut.* Privately printed, 2001.

Vickers, Raymond B. *Panic in Paradise: Florida's Banking Crash of 1926.* Tuscaloosa: University of Alabama Press, 1994.

Wallis, John Joseph, and Daniel K. Benjamin. "Public Relief and Private Employment in the Great Depression." *Journal of Economic History* 41, no. 1 (March 1981): 97–102.

Warner, Joe G. *Biscuits and 'Taters.* Bradenton, FL: Printing Professionals & Publishers, 1980.

Watson, Lynda. "Murphy Act Lands." Internal memorandum, Florida Department of Environmental Protection Tallahassee, December 19, 2007.

Whatley, Warren C. "Labor for the Picking: The New Deal in the South." *Journal of Economic History* 43, no. 4 (1983): 905–29.

Wynne, Debra, and Carolynn A. Washbon. *Judge Platt: Tales from a Florida Cattleman.* Gainesville: University of Florida Institute of Food and Agricultural Services, 1998.

Wynne, Nick, and Richard Moorhead. *Florida in World War II: Floating Fortress.* Charleston, SC: The History Press, 2010.

———. *Paradise for Sale: Florida's Booms and Busts.* Charleston, SC: The History Press, 2010.

INDEX

ABOUT THE AUTHORS

Nick Wynne is a retired college professor and the executive director emeritus of the Florida Historical Society. A prolific author, he has published, along with several coauthors and co-editors, more than twenty history books and five novels. He lives with his wife, Debra, in Rockledge, Florida, in a beautiful 1925 Mediterranean Revival house built during Florida's boom. This is his fifth book for The History Press.

Dr. Joe Knetsch, a historian, has published many books and over two hundred articles on Florida history, including his most recent book, *Florida in the Spanish-American War*, published by The History Press. He lives in Tallahassee with his wife, Linda, and his three felines: Magic, Oreo and Frankie.